THE H WORD

Beth, (my other daughter)
    Thank you for being
such a good friend and
for all you do. I hope this
book will be a blessing
to you.
                    I love you,

                    Vanessa
                    Headrick

VANESSA HEADRICK

THE H WORD

BRINGING

THE TRUTH OF

HOMOSEXUALITY

OUT OF THE

CLOSET

Tate Publishing & Enterprises

Published by Tate Publishing & Enterprises, LLC
127 E. Trade Center Terrace | Mustang, Oklahoma 73064 USA
1.888.361.9473 | www.tatepublishing.com

Tate Publishing is committed to excellence in the publishing industry. The company reflects the philosophy established by the founders, based on Psalm 68:11,
"The Lord gave the word and great was the company of those who published it."

Book design copyright © 2011 by Tate Publishing, LLC. All rights reserved.
Cover design by Kellie Southerland
Interior design by Joel Uber

Published in the United States of America

ISBN: 978-1-61739-739-4
1. Religion; Sexuality & Gender Studies
2. Religion; Christian Life, General
10.12.23

DEDICATION

*This book is dedicated to my family for their
unconditional love and prayers. To my mom, who
never gave up on me or the fight for my soul.*

A Word
from the Author

Before I write another word, I want to talk to those of you who know me. As I write this book, I am going to tell things and give examples that I have experienced. These examples are not about any single church or pastor. It is not my intention to point a finger at or embarrass anyone. It is my life and things I have had to deal with as a result of my past.

I hope you can see my heart and understand why I had to write what I have written. I was given an assignment by God. I pray it will accomplish his will and send a light of truth to those in darkness. I cannot apologize for doing what I believe the LORD has commissioned me to do.

In writing this book, the only reference books I am using are the King James Bible and the Strong's Exhaustive Concordance. I am telling you this because I do not want any secular ideas or opinions to be mixed with God's Word. I want anyone who reads this book to understand that I am in no way twisting, adding to, or taking from the truth, which is the word of God.

May God keep and bless you,
Vanessa

TABLE OF CONTENTS

FOREWORD

Many years ago, when I received a phone call that my daughter was making some very bad choices in life, I immediately took my Bible and fell to my knees. I told the LORD how I had failed and made many mistakes raising the child he had given me. It was then that I felt the Holy Spirit speak to my heart with the promise: "But I can correct mistakes." I have continued to pray and stand on that promise and want to tell you this book is verification that God never fails. I am very proud of Vanessa's accomplishment. I hope this book will give you hope for someone for whom you may be praying.

—Neva Everett, Vanessa's mom

INTRODUCTION

It is hard to find a family today who has not had to deal with the subject of homosexuality. Whether you are looking for answers for your children, grandchildren, aunt or uncle, cousin, or yourself, it is a subject that will, or has, touched your life.

Regardless of what you believe, homosexuality is a cause of controversy and confusion. It has divided numerous families, ruined relationships, and broken many hearts. It has been met with anger, frustration, grief, and alienation. Although the subject of homosexuality has been the topic of many discussions, debates, and much research, there are still unanswered questions, prejudice, hatred, and disagreements. Are people born that way? Is it a choice they made? Can they change? The list is endless.

It is my hope and prayer that this book will answer some of your questions, reunite families, mend broken hearts, and bridge the gap between the homosexual and the church. I am a spirit-filled Christian; yet, I lived over twenty years of my life as a homosexual. I think this gives me a valid voice in both areas.

If you are a homosexual, I want you to know I love you. It is not my intention, in any way, to show you in a negative light. You are important to God, and he loves you. He wants to change your name, reveal to you your purpose, and use you for his glory.

If you are a Christian or a minister, it's time you understand who these people are, where they are found in the Word of God, and who he created them to be. It's time we stop condemning them; instead, we need to reach out to them in love and compassion.

The Bible says in Romans 1:25 that "Satan takes the truth of God and turns it into a lie." It has been twelve years since the LORD commissioned me to "write it in a book." On January 1, 2010, he let me know "the time is now."

This is not only my story, but also the story of multitudes in the valley of decision. It's hard to make the right decision unless you know the truth about your options. I believe this book to be the truth behind the lie of homosexuality. I believe it will explain why Satan uses this particular lie, why he chooses who he chooses to attack, and the reward they are losing by believing the lie.

My goal is to bring the church and the homosexual together. Hostilities and misunderstandings cannot be overcome unless each group has insight and truth between them. It is impossible to effectively communicate with someone if you are not speaking the same language. The church, though unintentional, has been alienating the homosexual by their lack of understanding and the very verses they use to try and reach them.

It is late. Time is short. The Bible says there are fields ripe and ready for harvest. This field has been largely overlooked. You cannot harvest wheat with a cherry picker. You must be equipped with the appropriate tools. I believe this book will give you the tools needed before it is too late.

HE HAS ALWAYS BEEN WITH ME

I was born into a Pentecostal Holiness family. My grandma and grandpa were ministers for over sixty years. I was taught the Word of God from birth. My mom worked, and my grandma would babysit during the day. Every day, she would rock and sing to me, as I would fall asleep for my nap. Behind her rocking chair was a picture of Jesus standing and knocking on a door. As I fell asleep, I would look at the picture. It was on one of these days I spoke my first word: Jesus.

We were constantly going somewhere: to church, funerals, chicken dinners, visiting the sick, or home visitations. Each year, I would go with them for a week to camp meeting under a huge tent with nothing but dirt for a floor. . There would be people from all over the state coming together to camp, cook outdoors, and, of course—my favorite—visit the canteen. They were all there for one purpose. They were there to worship and praise God.

It was on one of these trips that I was sitting on my grandma's lap, staring out the car window, before the days of car seats and seat belts. I was looking up into the clouds, when suddenly, I saw a man kneeling by a bush that was on fire, but not burning. He had his sandals placed beside him. The bush was pretty and green, yet it refused to be burned by the fire. I asked my grandma who it was. Of course, she could not see him, but as I described to her what I saw, she knew I was seeing a vision. I can still hear her say, "My God, Walter. This baby has seen a vision." To this day, that vision has never faded from my memory, nor has it left my spirit. I am now forty-eight years old. I still do not understand why I saw Moses that day, nor do I understand why at various times throughout my life I have heard the LORD ask me,

"What's in your hand?" Call me a slow learner, but I do believe this book is a glimpse of what the LORD is preparing for me to do in his service.

God has done many miracles in my life. When I was three, I had asthma. At night, my mom would put a vaporizer beside my bed to help me breathe. It was not like the vaporizers we have today. You had to fill this vaporizer with boiling water. I got up during the night, tripped on the electrical cord, and pulled the vaporizer over, onto myself. It hit me about chest-level. Being a child, I did exactly what I shouldn't have done: I sat down in it and screamed for my mom. My mom panicked, wrapped me a blanket, and took me to my grandpa. When my grandpa opened the door, my mom threw me into his arms and said, "Here she is, Daddy. She's all burned up!" My grandpa instantly grabbed the Bible and fell to his knees, calling on God.

When they got me to the hospital, they had to remove the blanket. With it went my skin. I was in intensive care for ten days. The doctor prepared to do skin grafting surgery on my knee. The morning of the surgery, the doctor came in, unwrapped my knee, and, to his surprise, God had replaced the burned, dead skin with new skin. I do not have any scars anywhere on my body. Miracle.

Several times throughout my life, Satan has tried to blind me. My grandpa had bent a nail and used it as a hook on a fence. It just so happened that the height of this nail was the same height as my eyes from the ground. As I passed through the gate, the nail went in one side of my eye and wrapped around the back of my eyeball. There I stood, screaming for help. My mom looked out the kitchen window, saw me, and took off running through the house and fell into the middle of my grandma's bed, screaming hysterically, leaving me hanging on the fence. Thank God my aunt's ex-husband was there. He came out, took the nail off the fence, and took me to the hospital. The doctor said if they had twisted or tried to remove the nail, I would be blind today. Miracle.

Around the age of thirty, I was on the back of a motorcycle, or should I say "murdercycle." A retired, drunk preacher (how ironic) ran a stop sign and hit us. I came off the bike and slid down the hood of his truck. When he saw me, it scared him, and he slammed on the brakes, which threw me onto the road. It was the tenth of July; the road was hot. I couldn't get into a rolling position, but as I slid down the road, I remember reaching up and pulling down my shirt so no one would see my bra. I am my mother's daughter.

I received just shy of a hundred stitches from the outside of one eyebrow to the outside of the other eyebrow. I had a broken pubic bone, a broken pelvis, teeth knocked out, a hematoma on the back of my leg that grew to be the size of a soccer ball, and road rash, which covered the left side of my face and extended down to where my jeans began. Once again, I have no scars, except for a small one between my eyes from the hundred stitches. The police said if I had been wearing a helmet, the face shield would have either scalped me or blinded me. Miracle.

A couple of years later, I was at work. I was opening a container of some kind of chemical. The container exploded. The chemical burned my face and completely burned the lenses out of my safety glasses; however, not a drop got into my eyes. Again, you guessed it. I have no scars, and my vision was saved. Miracle.

There have been so many times the LORD, through his mercy, has spared me. I was shot in the head three times from a distance of three feet. The bullets fell to the ground. I did not see anything, but

I know there was an angel protecting me, keeping the bullets from hitting their mark. I was shot at, another time, and the gun jammed.

Once, while my friend and I were fishing, a tornado came straight down the bank at us. I turned to look at her; she was staring straight ahead of us instead of to our left, where the tornado was. I thought to myself, *What in the world could be more important than this tornado?* I turned to see what was so fascinating. I too saw something much more important. Jesus. He didn't say anything, but, needless to say, we completely forgot about the tornado. By the time we snapped back to reality, the tornado was gone. We looked at each other in disbelief. She asked if I had seen him too. I admitted I had. What a miracle.

As you can see, the Lord has been with me throughout my life. He has never left me, not even when I left him.

We do not see ourselves as God sees us. He knows what he placed within us while we were still in the womb.

> Before I formed thee in the belly I knew thee, and before thou camest forth out of the

> womb I sanctified thee, and I ordained thee a
> prophet unto the nations.
>
> Jeremiah 1:5

In this verse, God was speaking to Jeremiah, but the same is true of everyone. When he created us, he gave us gifts and talents to be used for his glory. I believe the LORD will follow us straight up to the gates of hell to keep us from going in, which is exactly what he has done for me.

He will also protect that which he has placed within us, as long as it is still useful. The sad thing is that some people outlive their usefulness. They continue to tell God no until after their appointed time to use their gifts has passed. At that time, there is no longer a use for them to remain on this earth. As bad as God hates to, at that point, he has to let them go into the eternity they choose.

Most would think with a background like mine that the choice of living for God versus living in sin would be an easy one. You would be wrong. I grew up surrounded by the Word of God, Christians, preachers, and church. I also grew up knowing there was something different about me. I did not grow up playing with dolls, dressing up in my mom's clothes, primping in front of the mirror, or dreaming of a wedding or a house with a white picket fence. Okay, maybe the house.

My dad was the classic underachiever and a serious diabetic, who paid absolutely no attention to his diet or sugar intake. He worked dead-end jobs as a mechanic; however, he could not keep a job for more than a couple of months at a time, due to his bad health. He would either get fired for absences or just stay home without calling in. If his sugar levels were too high, he would fly into an uncontrollable rage. He was also extremely jealous of me taking my mom's attention.

I was so scared of him that I began to stutter. I stuttered so badly that I couldn't ask for a drink of water. I believed, subconsciously, if I were quiet, it would not draw his attention to me. I can remember the frustration of knowing what I wanted to say but not being able to say it. I'd try to ask my mom for something and not be able to speak, which would so frustrate me I would begin to cry. She too would start crying because she didn't understand what I wanted. There we stood, looking at each other, both in tears. The mental picture is comical now, but it sure wasn't at the time.

Going to school was a whole different story. There was not a morning that my dread of school would not cause me to throw up. Forget about breakfast. My mom would drive me to school, and some mornings, she would have to physically remove me from the car. Of course, we would both be crying. She would have to drive off, leaving me standing beside the road, in tears. It was a terrible time in both of our lives.

Once I'd finally get to school, I had to deal with the cruelty of the other kids, though the kids were not as bad as the teachers. They knew I couldn't talk; yet, if anything needed to be read aloud, they would stand me in front of the class and force me to read. I'll never understand what they got out of doing that. It wasn't that everyone was taking their turn reading; I was the only one made to read. The things I was suffering at school only made my stuttering worse.

Although I dreaded going to school, home, for me, was not a place of comfort. I cannot remember ever sitting down at the dinner table and being able to finish a meal. From the moment we sat down, my dad would start in on me. He would pick and yell at me, finding fault with every bite I took and every move I made. I left the dinner table every night in tears. If he wasn't picking on me, he was arguing with my mom. I can remember, as a child, trying to position myself between them, thinking I was somehow protecting her.

I think my mom was even more miserable than I was. She, being a Pentecostal preacher's daughter, was torn between the church's teachings of forbidding divorce and not wanting to hurt my grandpa or his reputation. And, of course, there was the stigma she would have to face as a divorced woman in the church. Divorcing my dad would mean she would have to go against how she had been taught. Still, she knew divorcing my dad would be our only chance at having a real life.

At some point, my mom took me to a speech therapist. He told her if she would get me out of this environment, I'd be able to talk. With this information, and the fact that my dad began having an affair—the only justification for divorce in the eyes of the church—she finally divorced him.

Until now, I had grown up in fear. I was afraid of everything. I was afraid of school, my dad, of being home alone, and of going to bed. My mom would work all day, come home, fix dinner, try to keep peace in the house, and then, being totally exhausted, she

VANESSA HEADRICK

would sit on the edge of my bed every night until I fell asleep. What a life we had.

My mom got us an apartment, and at age twelve, she and I both felt like we had been let out of prison. We could laugh, talk, go out to eat, and have friends. For the first time in my life, I could sit down and eat a complete meal without anguish or tears.

For the first time, I felt safe. My speech began to steadily become clearer, and my fears, one by one, began to fade. The only downside was my mom had to work two jobs to support us. This meant, as an only child, more time alone. I was the original latch-key kid. She had to leave for work before I left for school and wouldn't get home until long after I did. She then would change clothes, grab a quick bite, and go back to work, which left me to spend the evenings alone. She would get home at bedtime. I was terrified of being at home alone. I remember sitting on the sofa with the television turned down as low as I could possibly turn it and still be able to hear at least part of what was being said. I was afraid I'd miss a noise. I would sit there, literally frozen in fear.

I didn't understand that God was trying to teach me and condition me to be who he created me to be. Neither did I understand that I was never really alone. He was always with me. Now, thirty-five years later, I know and understand. I was created to worship him, praise him, and minister to him. He was trying to teach me to be totally dependent on him and that he would never allow me to put anyone between us. This is, and always has been, my purpose.

THE SEEDS
HAD BEEN PLANTED

I was constantly pushed into dating by my friends who wanted to double date, and my family wanting to fix me up with boys in the church. I knew something about me was different. I had absolutely no desire to do anything with a guy, and anything sexual made me uneasy and nauseous.

I was confused because everyone else my age was crushing on this guy, that guy, and every guy in between. Just like everyone else, I was surrounded by sexual influences: music, TV, talk, etc. I tried to date a couple of times. However, I was simply uninterested. The pressure I felt was constant. Still, I had no desire—at least, no normal desire.

You see, Satan started when I was very young, convincing me I was different. Give me a choice between a doll and a BB gun, and I'd choose the gun. Give me a choice between playing with a bunch of little girls and playing ball with the boys, and I'd play ball, every time. Many people would just think I was a tomboy. The truth is, I was already confused at age six.

I can remember one time in particular that I went out to play ball. It was summer and the boys were hot, so they took their shirts off. I took mine off too. When I went home, my mom got on to me. She explained that I was not allowed to do that. I accepted her word for it but had no understanding why.

There had been a seed planted by my dad, who wanted a boy and didn't like me because I was a girl. Just like any kid, I wanted both of my parents to love me. In every way I could, I tried to please him. I worked on cars with him, rode his motorcycle with him, and went to work with him, trying to be what he wanted. As long as it was just he and I, we got along great. If I showed an interest in the things he liked, it made him feel like he wasn't missing out on not having a son. At least, this is what I thought as a child. Every time my mom would buy me a doll, he would take an ink pen and draw beards and mustaches on them. The only thing I ever remember him buying me was an electric race car track, which I suspect was really for himself. Needless to say, at a very young age, my wires were crossed.

When I was with my mom, I was at church, wearing frilly dresses and bouffant hairdos. I wanted to be the little girl she wanted, the little girl she could dress up and make over. But when I was with my dad, I tried to be the son he wanted, the son he never had. The older I got, the more I began to see myself as a boy. After all, if I were a boy, my parents' problems and my dad's anger would, in part, be appeased.

Believe it or not, I had two great passions. I loved the Word of God and knew he loved me. I also loved girls. I know that sounds impossible, but these were the two seeds planted in my spirit as a child. The Bible says you cannot serve two masters. This war raged within me, causing me to live in a state of confusion.

I loved the LORD but did not understand why he created me so messed up. I didn't understand my purpose. I didn't know there was a third lifestyle available. I knew I didn't want to go through life alone. I knew there was absolutely no way I could be with a guy. I wanted to fit in somewhere, but I didn't. I didn't fit in with the world because I had too much of God in me. I didn't fit in with the church because I had too much of the world in me. No one knew enough to tell me that I was okay, that maybe God created me this way for a purpose. Because of my loneliness and uneasiness around the opposite sex, sexual thoughts about other girls became my normal. I, after all, was comfortable around girls. The older I got, the thought of having a relationship with another girl seemed to just make sense. I accepted the realization that this was who I was created to be. I had no choice. I lived as a homosexual for over twenty years.

FINDING THE ANSWER

One day, I was at home alone, cleaning house. I don't know why, but my TV was on TBN without me realizing it. As I walked through the living room, I saw an attractive woman on the TV. I didn't know who she was; however, her looks caught my eye. God will use anything he has to in order to get your attention.

I stopped cleaning, went over to the TV, and turned the mute button off to see whom she was. It only took about thirty seconds before I was no longer looking at the flesh. She was singing, and boy was she anointed. I began to see something in her I had never seen before: Jesus. For the first time, I understood what it meant for someone to look like Jesus, act like Jesus, and talk like Jesus. I told the LORD, out loud, "If you can give me what she's got, I want it." I owe my salvation to her. Through her music, she taught me how to enter into worship. I was filled with the Holy Ghost while lying in the floor, on my face, singing with her CD.

It was at this point I had come to the end of myself. God had given me an ear to hear him. He had given me night visions or, if you will, holy dreams. He began to reveal to me glimpses of my future. The Holy Spirit taught me the Word of God; he showed me hidden mysteries written within the scriptures.

One day, as I was sitting in my living room, I cried out to God and asked him to show me where I was in his Word. I needed some answers as to why I was the way I was. I knew the answer was somewhere in the Bible, I had just never seen it or heard it. The Holy Spirit led me to Matthew 19:11–12. I knew this was the answer, but I only got part of the meaning. A day or two later, I heard the LORD say, "Write it in a book."

There are people who do not believe the LORD speaks to his children; however, it is biblical.

He that is of God heareth God's words: ye therefore hear them not, because you are not of God.

John 8:47

My sheep hear my voice, and I know them, and they follow me.

John 10:27

What I tell you in darkness, that speak ye in the light: and what you hear in the ear, that preach ye upon the housetops.

Matthew 10:27

There are times the LORD will show you something or tell you something for the future, then back you up and walk you through it, adding more and more pieces as you get closer to fulfilling it. It has taken me twelve years to walk this out.

It hasn't always been easy. I have fallen a couple of times. He has had to take things out of me, like jealousy, pride, fear, and much more. He has also had to teach me to forgive. He has taken people away from me that I thought would always be there. He has had to completely take me apart and put me back together. At first, I protested. I'd get mad at him, yell, and throw a fit. There have been times that all I could do was fall on the floor and cry until there were no more tears. But the further he has brought me, the easier it has become. Now if he says no, or that's got to go, I try to simply obey. Is he finished with me? No. He is never finished. It is a journey that lasts our entire lives. I will say it has all been worth it.

Now, I enjoy time alone with him. Instead of heartache, I have peace. Instead of depression and worry, I have joy. Instead of sin, I have him. I now understand why my journey has been so hard and why it was necessary. I understand why he made me the way he did. I had to go through it all to help others understand why they are different.

There is a well-known pastor on TV. I heard him make a comment that broke my heart. He said, "If the homosexual wants to go to hell, let them." I couldn't believe what I heard. It cut me like a knife. Sadly, this seems to be the attitude of a lot of preachers and Christians. Why? Jesus explained that in Matthew 19:11–12.

I would like to ask you to stop and ask the Lord to help you hear and receive what he has given me to share with you. It is a hard thing to accept. Jesus knew it would be; he warned us in his Word.

> But Jesus said unto them, (his disciples) all
> men cannot receive this saying, save they
> to whom it is given. For there are some
> eunuchs, which were so born from their
> mother's womb: and there are some eunuchs,
> which were made eunuchs of men: and there
> be eunuchs, which have made themselves
> eunuchs for the kingdom of heaven's sake.
> He that is able to receive it, let him receive it.
>
> Matthew 19:11–12

Wow, what a scripture. It is loaded with warnings, questions, and mystery.

Jesus always spoke in parables. The Bible says he did this so the ones who were serious about the Word would allow the Holy Spirit to explain it to them. The ones who were there for a show, just to see what he was doing or to look for a reason to find fault with him would not understand.

> And the disciples came, and said unto him,
> why speakest thou unto them in parables.
> He answered and said unto them, Because
> it is given unto you to know the mysteries
> of the kingdom of heaven, but to them it is
> not given.
>
> Matthew 13:10–11

When he says, "it is given to you," he means Christians. When he says, "to them, it is not given," he is speaking of anyone who is not seriously a follower of the Word.

If we take a close look at what Jesus said in Matthew 19:12, he describes three different types of eunuchs. Why society and evangelistic churches have seemed to ignore this, I don't know. There are, however, religions that do teach and have positions for eunuchs; though, they are not called by this name.

If you ask a Christian and most preachers what a eunuch is, they are quick to answer: a castrated man. They are right but fail to understand that this is not a complete definition. It is my intention to define each of the three types of eunuchs of which Jesus spoke. I am convinced when they are understood, broken hearts will be mended, families will be reunited, children will be taught truth, and many will be set free from believing Satan's all-consuming lie. People who have been told repeatedly that they are an abomination fit only for hell will be set free from this premise. They will realize how important they are and how much God loves them. For the first time, they will realize they were created differently on purpose, to be used for the glory of God and his will.

Eunuchs Defined

Jesus explained that there are three types of eunuchs. The first one I want us to look at is the one that is recognized by most churches. Throughout the Bible, you can find eunuchs holding various positions, both in the Old and New Testaments. They are eunuchs who have been castrated (made that way by men). They were primarily used to watch over the king's harems. They were totally trusted because of their inability to have sex. In Esther 2:3–14, we see they are also called "chamberlains." In Daniel 1:3, we find a eunuch as the king's attendant. In Acts 8:27, we see a eunuch who was the queen of Ethiopia's head treasurer. There are other examples and offices held by eunuchs in the Bible. You can see, just from these examples, they were highly trusted and valuable to the leaders of the time.

The second type of eunuchs is men and women who chose to live unmarried and celibate throughout their lives in order to concentrate entirely on the things of God. The best example we have of this today is from the Catholic Church. Priests and nuns willingly give their lives to study, worship, and live a life of self-sacrifice unto God. We have seen that there are some who fail. However, there have been thousands of others who have successfully denied their flesh in God's service. You have to admit, these people should be admired and rewarded for their dedication.

There are several people in the Bible who were this type of eunuch. Let's look at just a couple who are best known. Keep in mind, these people were born with normal sex drives and attractions; yet, they chose God instead.

First, let's take a look at Paul. Paul wrote two-thirds of the New Testament; he also established many churches, teaching and preaching the resurrected Christ. He took four evangelistic journeys, the fourth reaching all the way from Jerusalem to Rome. Paul spoke several times about choosing to live as a eunuch.

> For I would that all men were even as I myself.
>
> 1 Corinthians 7:7

> But I would have you without anxiety. He that is unmarried careth for the things that belong to the LORD, How he may please the LORD. But he that is married careth for the things that are of the world, how he may please his wife.
>
> 1 Corinthians 7:32–33

> The unmarried woman careth for the things of the LORD, that she may be holy both in body and in spirit, but she that is married careth for the things of the world, how she may please her husband.
>
> 1 Corinthians 7:34

We can see by these scriptures that Paul willingly gave himself—body, mind, and spirit—to be used by God. It was his teaching to men and women that if they would do the same, they could have a closer, unrestricted, uncompromising relationship with the LORD. There are people who will argue that only men were, or can be, eunuchs. Yet, in the scriptures we just read, we see how Paul made a point to include women.

Now, let's take a look at John. John was one of Jesus' disciples. The Bible paints a picture of a special closeness between Jesus and John. It is recorded five times in Scripture how Jesus loved him. As Jesus hung on the cross, dying, the Bible says, in John 19:26, that Jesus looked down and saw his mother, Mary, and John. He commissioned John to become a son to his mother. From that day on, Mary lived with John in his home. Complete trust and dedication is shown in this relationship.

We have to ask ourselves: What was this bond between Jesus and John? What about John would cause Jesus to trust him to take care of his mother? What would make John willing to take on such a responsibility? Why is it recorded repeatedly how Jesus loved him?

Could it be Jesus knew that John's sacrifice and love for him was so strong, so consuming, that he was willing to choose the life of a eunuch for his glory? This is not recorded in the Bible like it is with Paul. However, we, through Scripture, know other disciples were married; yet, of John, it is not so. John eventually was exiled to the isle of Patmos for preaching Jesus. He lived there, alone, writing Revelation. What an honor for his life of dedication and love for the LORD.

Peter was also one of Jesus' disciples. Although the Bible tells us that Peter was married, it is believed the reason he was eventually crucified was because of his constant and insistent preaching of abstinence. This teaching was particularly accepted by the women of that time, which, needless to say, greatly angered the men to the point of them wanting him dead.

The best description the Bible gives of a godly eunuch is Daniel. In II Kings 20, we read of Hezekiah, who had disobeyed God.

> And of thy sons that shall issue from thee, which thou shalt beget, shall they take away; and they shall be eunuchs in the palace of the king of Babylon.
>
> II Kings 20:18

In the first chapter of Daniel, this event is described. Daniel, Hananiah, Mishael, and Azariah, better known as Shadrach, Meshach, and Abednego, were described as excellent and favored, full of wisdom, knowledge, and understanding. Verse nineteen says there was none found like these four; they were ten times better than all those who stood before the king prior.

Most of us know the story of their refusal to worship or bow the knee to anyone but God. Shadrach, Meshach, and Abednego were thrown into a fiery furnace yet came out without being burned. Daniel refused to obey an order not to pray to his God. He was thrown into a lion's den but came out without harm. They refused to allow the Babylonian ways to change their dedication, love, and obedience to God.

Their examples changed an entire kingdom. When King Nebuchadnezzar saw their faith and the wondrous miracles displayed by the hand of God, he made a decree that all flesh, in his kingdom, would serve their living God.

> 26 I make a decree, that in every dominion of my kingdom men tremble and fear before the God of Daniel: for he is the living God, and steadfast for ever, and his kingdom that which shall not be destroyed, and his dominion shall be even unto the end.

27 He delivereth and rescueth, and he wor-keth signs and wonders in heaven and in earth.

The Bible says Daniel was greatly beloved by God. While it is true, God loves everyone; he richly rewards those who are willing to live their lives as a sacrifice unto him. The best way I can describe this is if you have children, you love them all the same; however, you may have a special bond or closeness with one that you don't have with the others, usually due to common interests and similar personalities. It is the same with our Heavenly Father.

When we, who were created to live in the likeness of our Father, begin to take a stand and allow him to change us and fulfill our destiny, it touches a reserved place within his heart—to know that we choose him and love him above all others, above all this world has to offer.

In each of these examples, we see how God used and blessed these eunuchs with not only his super-natural wonders but also an intense personal relationship between them and himself. He longs to do the same today in the lives of those who he has chosen to be his own.

EUNUCH #3

Eunuch #3 is the truth that contradicts the lie of homosexuality. When the LORD allowed me to see myself in Matthew 19:11–12, I began to search and read all I could find on these verses. I have been able to find eunuch #1, the castrated male, in every written definition and translation. I have found only a few examples of eunuch #2, the choice to live sacrificially unto the LORD by living celibate. I have never, in the last twelve years, found a definition or translation of eunuch #3.

Eunuch[1] in Strong's Exhaustive Concordance gave me a Hebrew definition that shocked me.

eunuch - reb-aw-baw' - many, million, x
multiplied, ten thousands

This completely blew my mind when I first read it.
If you are a Christian, there is one thing I'm sure
you know; God does not change. If it was his will
and design to create and have need of eunuchs at
the time Jesus spoke these words, then it must be
his will and design today. He would not have created or spoken of them unless he had a purpose for
them. With seven and a half billion people on the
planet today, we must ask ourselves, *Where are these
millions of eunuchs today?* To me, this was confirma-
tion of what I had been led to understand through
the Holy Spirit. It also instantly brought to my mind
this passage.

> Put ye in the sickle, for the harvest is ripe:
> get you down; for the press is full, the fats
> overflow; for their wickedness is great. Mul-
> titudes, multitudes, in the valley of decision:
> for the day of the LORD is near in the valley
> of decision.
>
> Joel 3:13–14

One night, as I slept, the LORD gave me a dream. I was sitting on the porch of a house. As I looked out, all I could see were fields of golden wheat blowing in the wind. I heard a voice behind me say, "The time of harvest is come." I knew, in my dream, that my grandpa had planted these fields; yet, it was up to me to harvest them. I believe the fields I saw that night represented the millions in the valley of decision. For me, it meant the million x multiplied. Those who have been lied to by Satan needed to know the truth.

There are millions of people who profess to be homosexual. They have repeatedly explained they were born that way. They are half right. They were born different. The church does not understand how this can be. Because it is not their own experience, they simply dismiss this claim. They fanatically deny that this is true. Let's think back to what Jesus said in Matthew 19:11: "If this word is not for you, you will not understand it." Every word of Jesus is truth, and this is why the church, Christians, and sinners alike can agree; they cannot relate or understand.

Satan will always attack you in the exact areas of which God intends for you to be blessed and used for his glory. Throughout my life, I have been repeatedly attacked in three specific areas.

First, my vision. I have told you how Satan has tried, over and over, to blind me. If he had been successful, this would not have meant I could not serve the LORD. I believe it was more symbolic; he knowing that I knew the scriptures.

Where there is no vision, the people perish.
Proverbs 29:18

I don't know for sure, but it may have also affected my ability to receive dreams and visions of which the LORD has blessed me with the ability to see.

Second, my speech. As I have also told you, I couldn't speak clearly until I was twelve years old. Before I was saved, when I was in a stressful situation, my speech impediment would return. This attack was Satan's way of trying to keep me quiet. It was his way of assuring I would not have a voice to speak and spread the word of God.

Finally, my horrific fear of being alone. This was Satan's ultimate attack. This single fear is what he used to convince me to forsake God and accept homosexuality.

> For God hath not given us the spirit of fear;
> but of power, and of love, and of, a sound
> mind.
>
> 2 Timothy 1:7

Anytime you become bound by something that Satan tries to put on you—in my case, fear—you leave yourself open for more bondage. You will always end up in a worse state, for me, homosexuality. Because homosexuality is such a consuming sin, taking over the life of whoever is affected, it is next to impossible for someone who is homosexual to be reformed. I use that word lightly.

There are many programs, sex therapists, psychiatrists, etc., who have worked with people, to little or no avail. It is impossible to be changed without Christ. I know there are a few who, after working one of these programs, claim to be changed. Deep inside, they are still struggling. While they may do well for a season, they are still fighting their feelings.

For those of you who would disagree and claim you are totally free, save your breath. I don't believe you; after all, I am you. If not for the LORD, it still would be a daily struggle. I tried it your way. It doesn't work, not completely. Yes, you may be denying yourself, stuffing your desires, putting on a smile, and even getting married. The truth is, somewhere inside you, the seed remains.

> If the Son (Jesus) therefore shall make you free, ye shall be free indeed.
>
> John 8:36

Without Jesus, you may consider yourself free, but you do not have the indeed. The root, or seed, still remains. If you would be totally honest with yourself, you would know I am telling you the truth. The indeed requires a daily, close, personal, relationship with the LORD. You may be able to last awhile without him, but eventually, you will fail.

As I said in the beginning of this book, there was something different about me, even as a young child. I can remember back to age two. I can tell you the first crush I ever had on a girl was in kindergarten. Many people do not understand that Satan does not play fair. It doesn't seem right that he should be able to attack a defenseless child. I agree. It is, however, biblical. Mark 9:17–27 tells a story about a father who brought his son to Jesus to be prayed for. The boy was being attacked by Satan. Jesus asked the father how long it had been happening.

And he (Jesus) asked his (the boys) father,
How long is it ago since this came to him?
And he said, of a child.

Mark 19:21

A child does not have the ability to fight for itself; neither does it understand right from wrong until it is taught. The problem is, by the time most people begin to teach their children about sexual things, Satan already has the child believing, if not convinced of, a lie. God even calls it a lie in his Word.

Who changed the truth of God into a lie, and worshiped and served the creature more than the Creator, who is blessed forever.

Romans 1:25

This verse makes it clear if you are focused more on the flesh (man or woman) and allowing that focus to control you, you are worshiping the creature. You are not focusing on the Creator, God.

Nehemiah was commissioned by God to repair the wall of Jerusalem, which had been destroyed by Nebuchadnezzar. The wall had been partially rebuilt, but construction had been stopped by Artaxerxes (this is can be read in Ezra 4). As Nehemiah began to rebuild the burnt walls, he was instantly met with opposition. His enemy, Sanballet, asked him a very important question.

> Will they revive the stones out of the heaps of rubbish which are burned?
>
> Nehemiah 4:2

The Bible is full of types and shadows or examples and comparisons. As you read the Bible, you discover the Jews are God's chosen people; their rejection of Jesus as the Messiah and his crucifixion allows for others—Gentiles (you and me)—to be grafted into the family of God. When you read a promise in the Bible given to the Jewish people, you as a Christian are also included in that promise. It is the same when you read of the temple; it can also include the church. Because of this, we can ask ourselves, as the church, "Will we revive the stones out of the heaps of rubbish that are burned?"

As we go through life, things can happen that leave us hurt, wounded, cast down, and changed. Satan takes this opportunity to fill us with depression, bitterness, and the inability to forgive. When this happens, many people quit the church and blame God, and thus, become burnt. When it happens to people who have not been taught the Word of God or ever been a part of a church, they simply give up and often see themselves as unloved and unwanted.

Our world today is filled with people who are burnt. We have grown accustomed to the belief that every problem can be dealt with by giving it a label and throwing medication at it. We have pills for everything from fear and depression to compulsions, such as biting our fingernails or picking at our skin. It doesn't matter what the problem is, there is a medication for it and a doctor eager to pass it out.

Many of these things are simply attacks of our minds by Satan. Since we no longer believe God's Word as a nation, we are uneducated about how to use the power and weapons of the Holy Spirit to overcome these attacks.

> My people are destroyed for lack of knowledge: because thou hast rejected knowledge, I will also reject thee.
>
> Hosea 4:6

If you think back thirty years ago, we did not have all these so-called illnesses. Why? We were still basically a godly nation. Now if you believe in Jesus Christ, your right to worship is slowly being stripped away. In the verse we just read, we can see why. When we, as a nation, begin to reject God—taking him out of everything from schools to courtrooms to Christmas—he, in turn, begins to reject us. When this happens, the covering of security that he provided for us begins to be removed, leaving us open for attack physically and spiritually, which is why we are experiencing more attacks on this country and on our health than ever before. Don't misunderstand me. I believe in doctors, hospitals, and medication. However, some of these "medical" conditions may be the result of demonic attacks. These people have been hurt, burnt. They are suffering mental attacks. Without knowledge of the weapons available to them through Christ Jesus and his Holy Spirit, they are defenseless.

> For we wrestle not against flesh and blood, but against principalities, against powers, against the rulers of the darkness of this world, against spiritual wickedness in high places.
>
> Ephesians 6:12

> For the weapons of our warfare are not carnal, but mighty through God to the pulling

down of strongholds; Casting down imagina-
tions, and every high thing that exalteth itself
against the knowledge of God, and bringing
into captivity every thought to the obedience
of Christ.

2 Corinthians 10:4–5

Without people having knowledge of what is available to them, they are open and helpless against these
attacks of Satan. So they try to fight back through
the use of drugs, both legal and illegal. They try
to smoke them away, snort them away, shoot them
away, and drink them away. They are losing the war.
Regardless of what background you come from, we
are being changed and hardened by our experiences
and these attacks. More and more of us each day are
becoming burnt stones.

The only hope for us to return and come to the
knowledge of God and his purpose for our lives is
for someone, in Christ's love and compassion, to
reach out and begin to polish and restore us to our
intended place on the wall of godliness. We need to
be taught what is available to us through the Word
of God. The surprising thing about a burnt stone is,
when picked up, cared for, polished, and placed back
on the wall, it shines brighter than all other stones.

ALL HAVE SINNED

Satan will always take the things belonging to God and twist them, pervert them, and use them for his own glory. Jesus said in John 8:44, "Satan is a liar, the father of it, and there is no truth in him." We know because of these words that any lie originates from Satan.

We all know there are different kinds of lies. There are social lies, lies we tell ourselves, and don't forget the white lies. The name alone is deceiving. The word *white* brings to mind something pure and clean, which is exactly how Satan deceives us into believing it is not a sin.

I have heard it said that it is impossible to go through an entire day without lying. Many times, people lie and don't even realize it. We have grown so accustomed to stretching or bending the truth, that it seems to come out of our mouths before we know it. We don't give it a second thought.

I never thought of myself as a liar. However, when I first became a Christian and began to learn about bridling my tongue, I was shocked and amazed. I knew what the Bible said about lying. It says that God hates a liar, and in Revelation 21:8, it plainly tells the future of anyone who lies.

> But the fearful, and unbelieving, and the abominable, and the murders, and the whore mongers, and sorcerers, and idolaters, and all liars shall have their part in the lake which burneth with fire and brimstone.
>
> Revelation 21:8

It is also how Satan blinds us to our own sins. He tells us our sins are not as grievous as those of others.

Why am I going into such detail about lies? We have to understand that whatever our struggle in life may be, it is based on a lie. The first words Satan ever spoke to humanity in the Garden of Eden was a twisted, fragmented truth of what God actually had said. Everything he has ever spoken has been, at best, a partial truth, if not a blatant lie. The Bible says in Hosea 4:6, "My people are destroyed for lack of knowledge". The word knowledge[1], in Hebrew, means to lack instruction and comprehension, to be unaware, and to be lied to.

Here is the point I want everyone to understand. Unless you read and study the Bible, you do not know what is truth or what is a lie, so you fall for anything Satan tells you. All of us wrestle with things in this life. No one is exempt. The people who judge and condemn the homosexuals fail to realize they are expecting that person to live a life that they themselves are unable to live. A life without any misled beliefs.

Regardless of what we believe, we have to come to the realization that any prejudice or condemnation is Satan lying to us. It doesn't matter who we are; Romans 3:23 says, "All have sinned, and come short of the glory of God". Satan has lied to many people, convincing them they are somehow better, purer, or cleaner than the homosexual. This is not true. We can all point a finger at the sins of those around us, and it may for a while take the attention off of us; however, it will never distract or confuse God's view of us.

> For whosoever shall keep the whole law, and yet offend (stumble) in one point, he is guilty of all.
>
> James 2:10

We must realize we are all the same. We are all on the devil's hit list and struggling with something he has told us. The homosexual is no different. They are dealing the best they can with the hand life has dealt them. Yet, most of society's judgment in the area of morals is directed towards the homosexual. Why? I believe it is because of their lack of understanding and compassion for these people who have fallen for the lie they have been told. It may not be the lie you fight with, but, as the verse we just read declares, we are all equally guilty in God's eyes.

Another reason people are uneasy with the subject of homosexuality, and why they are often judged so harshly, is the mystery of the lifestyle. There have been many misconceptions surrounding this way of life, and we all know the imagination can come up with some wild tales. So, let me help put some of these misconceptions to rest.

For many years it was believed to be dangerous to allow children to be alone with a homosexual because of fear of molestation. This is completely untrue. They are no more attracted to children than heterosexuals.

It is thought they are all out to recruit heterosexuals into their lifestyle. While there are extremists in all walks of life, the majority is not this way. They are simply trying to make the relationship they are in a happy one.

I have had people tell me they thought all homosexuals were attracted to everyone of the same sex. To me this is crazy thinking. Just like anyone else, they are attracted to someone who interests them and with whom they are comfortable.

I have had heterosexual friends who were surprised to learn that most homosexuals are in, or are wanting, a monogamist relationship. They want a stable home and family, which is why they want the right to marry.

Some people are amazed to discover that most homosexuals are good, hard working, and caring people with the same goals as the heterosexual. They are not looking for trouble or drama. They are working toward, and looking for, ways to better their lives.

It is my hope these truths will allow you to see the homosexual in a different light. As I said earlier, we are all the same. We all long for the same things—a home, someone to love us, a family, and a sense of belonging and acceptance. The only things that make us different are the things we struggle with and the lies we have been told; whether the problem is with weight, lying, lust, anger, depression, or homosexuality, we are all in a fight for our souls.

> He that turneth away his ear from hearing
> the law, even his prayer shall be abomination.
> Proverbs 28:9

In this verse, the Hebrew meaning for the word law[1] is teaching, information, or instruction. What does this mean? It means if anyone receives Godly teachings and refuses to change their wrong or ungodly opinions, attitudes, or judgments accordingly, it is seen as sin by God, and they will be held accountable. God views people who judge others, just as guilty as the person they are judging. I am not saying we should not take a stand against sin; however, we are to search our hearts, making sure it is the sin we hate while still able and willing to love the sinner, else we too become guilty.

WE MUST CHANGE THE MESSAGE

I know, for a fact, with or without homosexuality, I was not born with an attraction to the opposite sex. This does not mean that I was born homosexual. It means I was born different. In our world, we are conditioned by society to believe everyone is a sexual being. This is not true. It is, however, how we are leaving the door open for Satan to attack our children. Even when our children are young, we often notice them displaying characteristics of the opposite sex. Most of the time, we ignore it, thinking they will grow out of it; sometimes, they do. More often than not, it just becomes worse the older they become.

Finally, they reach puberty, and parents act shocked, hurt, and disgusted when confronted with the announcement of their child's homosexuality. If truth be told, they knew something was wrong. Still, they refused to accept it. Then, when their child comes out of the closet, many are punished, disowned, and kicked out. Parents cry uncontrollably, like making them feel guilty will somehow change them. What we are actually doing is handing them over to Satan. By kicking them out or disowning them, we are doing exactly what Satan wants us to do: we are sending them to his house. Rest assured, he will accept them.

I have heard some say, "Well, I won't have that in my house." To those who would say such a thing, guess what? It has been in your house since your child was three or four years old. It has always amazed me how parents seem to be loving and attentive: they set curfews, go to their child's school functions, and carpool them and their friends. They are totally devoted until the H word, homosexuality, is spoken. Now, instead of tucking them into bed, they are forcing them into someone else's, by denying them their own home and family. Nothing has changed for the child; they are who they have always been. The parents, on the other hand, have totally changed overnight. This only adds to the child's confusion and pain, which causes them to become irreverent and burnt. Parents are supposed to be examples of God in their child's life. By acting in ways I have described, the child believes it is also God's reaction.

Thank God that he is an understanding, loving, compassionate Father. People often have a false image of who God is as our Father because of the example they have been shown by their earthly fathers. God is long-suffering and forgiving. Our heavenly Father will never give up on us or leave us. We can never shock him or confuse him. Often, we may disappoint him. Still, he continues to watch and wait for us to return to him. He loves us unconditionally.

I am ashamed to say the church is little, if any, help in this area. Instead of reaching out to the homosexual and loving them, they are repeatedly told it is a lifestyle they chose, they are going to hell, and they are an abomination. I wish some minister or Christian would explain to me how this would make anyone want to give themselves to God and become like their accusers.

Let me make this clear to anyone who has ever said or believed someone who said that they chose this lifestyle. They did not. You tell yourselves that to make it easier for you to dismiss the problem for which you have no answer. The church believes and preaches this, for if they didn't, it would somehow mean God must have messed up, which, of course, is untrue.

There are some who are so addicted and bound to sex that they call themselves "bisexuals." They don't care whom they are with, as long as they are with someone. This is done by choice. If they have an attraction to the opposite sex, then they have no need for a same-sex relationship. There are also a few homosexuals who do have attractions to the opposite sex, though this attraction is not as strong as the same-sex attraction. These people are usually the ones who were molested, causing confusion in their identity or fear toward the sex that molested them. These can be set free from this confusion and fear and live life as a heterosexual by the power of God. They would be eunuch #1: made that way by man.

A homosexual with no attraction to the opposite sex has no choice. They did not choose to be an outcast. They did not choose to be hated, made fun of, alienated, and abused. Ask yourself the question: Why would anyone choose to be disowned by their families, be discriminated against in society, or be considered less than human by haters? Why would they choose to live a life that would never allow them to have families of their own or the small things that heterosexuals take for granted? Heterosexuals don't think twice about holding hands while going for a walk or sitting with their arm around the person they love at dinner.

Why would they choose such a hard life if they didn't feel as if they had no other choice? Isn't life hard enough without all these extra hardships? Every time someone says, "They chose that lifestyle," they are proving the words of Jesus to be true. You do not have a clue; you don't understand the first thing about it. If you do not understand, you should at least try to be concerned enough about these people's souls to find out the truth.

I understand a preacher's need to explain to homosexuals they are living in sin and on the road to hell. It is their calling. But please hear me: you are losing the people you are trying to reach *instantly* when you preach any of these three things.

1. Sodom and Gomorrah were destroyed because of homosexuality. This is not entirely true.

> Because the cry of Sodom and Gomorrah is great, and because their sin is very grievous:
>
> Genesis 18:20

This is the explanation the LORD gave as to why he was going to destroy Sodom and Gomorrah.

Grievous[1], in the Hebrew means *numerous or many*. Nowhere in the Bible does it say he destroyed them for any one type of sin. He destroyed them for all manner of sin.

In every sermon I have ever heard on homosexuality, the minister refers to Genesis 19, in which two angels entered Sodom to deliver Lot and his family. When they entered Lot's house, the men of Sodom surrounded the house and commanded Lot to send them out so they could rape them. This is the passage they take and why they say Sodom was destroyed because of homosexuality, never mind there was also the sin of rape involved, showing not only the wide range of sin but also the total lack of fear and reverence for God. I want us to look at a passage of this story.

Bring them out unto us, that we may know them.

Genesis 19:5

I pray you, brethren, do not so wickedly.

Genesis 19:7

There is not a Holiness preacher in the world that does not believe Jerusalem is the Holy Land and should be protected at all cost. I agree with them; however, the exact same event happened in Jerusalem.

Bring forth the man that came into thine house, that we may know him.

Judges 19:22

My brethren, nay, I pray you, do not so wickedly.

Judges 19:23

This is almost the same event, word for word. The difference is, the passages in Judges occurred, approximately two miles from Jerusalem. Never once have I ever heard any preacher say that Jerusalem should have been destroyed. So we have to ask the obvious question: Why did God destroy Sodom but did not destroy Jerusalem, if Sodom was destroyed because of the homosexuality? The answer is, this was not the only sin for which Sodom and Gomorrah were destroyed. They were destroyed, as I said, for the abundance and combination of all sins, grievous sin.

2. Stop calling the homosexual an abomination. The sin is an abomination, not the individual. The Bible lists several things that are considered abominations.

> These six things doth the LORD hate, yea, seven are an abomination unto him: A proud look, a lying tongue, and hands that shed innocent blood, An heart that deviseth wicked imaginations, feet that be swift in running to mischief, A false witness that speaketh lies, and he that soweth discord among brethren.
>
> Proverbs 6:16–19

There are others in the Bible. Yet, I have never heard a sermon in which any of these were called an abomination—only homosexuality. Why is this? I believe it is because we as humans do not have the ability to see all sin the same. We truly believe there are some sins worse than others.

3. The quickest way to turn a homosexual off to the message you are trying to convey is to say they chose that lifestyle. The second you say this you lose them. Why? They know it is untrue, and if they know this is untrue, then how can they believe anything else you say?

How would you like it if someone got up and told you that God hates you so much that he destroyed cities, trying to get rid of people like you? Then they tell you that you are guilty of the worst sin known to man, and it's all because you're stubborn, hardheaded and because you refuse to stop being you. How would you feel? I seriously doubt that you would be filled with the warm fuzzies. By saying things of which we do not understand their effect, we are convincing the homosexual that this is the heart of the LORD toward them: hard and cold, without compassion, interest, or understanding. While this seems to be an accurate picture of many Christians and ministers, it is not an accurate picture of Jesus. When we stand before him, I believe we are going to have to explain our lack of compassion and love for these people and why we aided Satan in hardening their hearts against him.

Another verse, often used, when trying to minister to the homosexual is taken completely out of context.

> So God created man in his own image, in the image of God created he him; male and female created he them. And God blessed them, and God said unto them, Be fruitful and multiply, and replenish the earth, and subdue it:
>
> Genesis 1:27–28

God was not saying everyone who comes out of the womb must reproduce. If you believe that, then you do not believe Paul, which means you do not believe two-thirds of the New Testament. God was telling Adam and Eve what he created them for. There was no homosexual in the picture. At that time, there had never been a homosexual. That was the furthest thing from God's mind.

Let's try talking to them from a heart of compassion and mercy. We need to also let them know that we have a heart to understand and an eagerness to accept them into our lives, homes, and churches. We can't expect them to give up their friends, activities, and lifestyle without becoming their friends, inviting them to our activities, and making them feel like they have a place where they are welcome and accepted.

They know if the word being given is out of disgust or from the heart. Talk to them where they live. Tell them the truth. Educate them on the spirit of bondage. Build them up, and tell them who they can become in the kingdom of God. Let them know there is hidden treasure inside them and God created them with purpose.

Let me make it clear. There are people who are born without the desire for sex. Satan's lies and the pressures of a sexual society have caused many of them to accept the comfort and companionship they find in a same-sex relationship. God did not make a mistake by creating them. He created them to be his own. He created them to love him above all else, to be totally dependent upon him, and to be available to him. They are to live their lives pure, a holy vessel, married only to himself. They were born to live the ultimate walk of faith, to be in the world but not of the world, giving themselves and their lives completely over to God. They are to be a living sacrifice, whose only desire is the LORD. What an honor.

WHO'S WHO?

You may ask: If it is true that God created these people for himself, what happened? How did they become homosexual? The answer is fairly simple. First, I must say I do not believe all homosexuals were created to live the life of a eunuch. Just as Jesus explained how there are three types of eunuchs, you must understand there are also three types of homosexuals. True to the form of a eunuch, there are some who choose the lifestyle even though they have the ability to be attracted to the opposite sex. There are also some who, due to being molested, have grown confused, feeling as if their sexuality was taken from them. Then, there are those who were born without any attraction to the opposite sex. It is this group that, without Christ, grows to believe they were born homosexual due to the reoccurring thoughts planted in their minds by Satan throughout their lives and the human need to be confirmed and feel loved.

It is also this group whom I believe Jesus was referring to in Matthew 19:11. They were created on purpose, with purpose. Just as the Levites of the Old Testament were, from birth, chosen and designated to fulfill the offices of the temple, so too are these lost eunuchs of today, born to be in service to the LORD.

Paul made it very clear in 1Corinthians 7:35, the reason why this lifestyle is so important. He described it as the availability to attend unto the LORD without distraction. Although Paul seemed to impress the need for this to be taught in the church, it is one of his messages that has not been kept alive in mainstream denominations, except for Catholicism. It is absolutely vital this message is resurrected and preached as a legitimate and important lifestyle.

I am not suggesting there should be designated offices for a eunuch held in churches. I am, however, pleading the importance of the nonsexual lifestyle to be taught and celebrated as an available and important way of life—a life unencumbered by the cares of the world and completely available to the LORD to fulfill whatever calling they are anointed for, whether it be a missionary, disaster relief worker, preacher, teacher, prophet, etc.

I am going to ask you to take a trip with me. If you can, think back to when you were sixteen or seventeen years old. Everyone around you is dating, everywhere you look and everything you hear is screaming sex at you. You cannot understand what the big deal is, because you have never had any thoughts or feelings toward anyone of the opposite sex.

Someone asks you out on a date; although you really have no desire to go, you feel like you have to just to prove yourself to family and friends. Your date is nice enough, but when you kiss goodnight, you feel as if you have just kissed your brother or sister inappropriately. You are totally repulsed, a little nauseous, and completely uncomfortable in your own skin. You actually feel gay for the first time.

You're now safe at home alone in your room; questions, fear, and confusion flood your mind. You can't tell anyone. What would they think? You can't stand the thoughts of your future: a life of loneliness, no one to share things with, no family of your own, no one to love, and no one to love you. So, you decide to try again and again. Each time the outcome is the same, if not worse.

The time comes when you are confronted with a decision. You meet someone of the same sex whom you feel you have known all your life. You have a great time together. You have never felt as close to anyone as you do to this person. They make a sexual comment to you, and though you have never admitted it to anyone, you know you have had these same thoughts and feelings. Suddenly, the future doesn't seem so hopeless. What do you do?

This scenario plays out each and every day. Without God in your life and the Holy Spirit living within you, the choice is an easy one; you choose what you think will bring you happiness and fulfillment. You have never heard of a eunuch or a nonsexual lifestyle. As far as you know, there is no third choice. You are faced with a life of loneliness, discontentment, and uncertainty. You do not understand how you were set up by the devil. This person did not just wonder into your life. You don't realize the previous thoughts you had were whispered into your spirit by the enemy or how they have taken root and began to grow within your heart and mind. You have no understanding of how a spirit of homosexuality has attached itself to you and is calling out to other like spirits (the world calls this gaydar). All you know is, you have found someone to go through life with, and for now, you are happy.

This scene will continue, and Satan will quickly take our loved ones hostage, unless we give them an alternative. They need to know there is someone who loves them more than life. He longs for them and desires to have a one-on-one relationship with them. He is their soul mate, the only one who can complete them. He is the one they were created to walk with, talk with, share life with, and love throughout all eternity. He alone can fulfill their purpose, desires, and destiny.

Remember, I told you that Satan attacks people in the area of their purpose. When God placed within us our gifts, talents, and callings, we were still in the womb. We are born with no memory of these things. We do not know what our purpose is. Satan, however, does know our purpose. This is how he knows how to attack us.

We know this is true by looking at Moses and Jesus: the greatest two deliverers that have ever lived.

When each of them was born, Satan immediately began to try and have them destroyed. Though they were born at different times, the kings of their day sent out decrees to destroy all male babies. Satan knew what was placed inside them and tried to stop them before they were able to accomplish their destinies.

The same is true today. He begins to attack us before we realize who we are intended to become. What better way to stop someone who was created to live holy and pure before the Lord than to create in them the complete opposite, both in man's eyes and in God's eyes. He starts when we are so young that by the time we become teenagers, we are totally convinced we have no option. We have no previous memory of who God created us to be; therefore, we believe we were born that way. There is no choice to be made. The only choice is whether to let others know who we are or live what we consider to be the lie—the life of a heterosexual.

Genius, isn't it? Take someone who was intended to live holy and pure before the Lord and convince them of a lie, which leads them to believe they were created unholy and impure. In their mind, the only one responsible is God.

Who changed the truth of God into a lie, and
worshiped the creature more than the creator.

Romans 1:25

Of course, they are going to worship the creature.
After all, it is the Creator who made them the way
they are.

There is one little problem with this masterpiece
of Satan's. It is called *redemption*.

Teaching us that, denying ungodliness and
worldly lusts, we should live soberly, righ-
teously, and godly, in this present world.

Titus 2:12

Jesus gave himself so that we may be rescued from
the lie of Satan. When Jesus gave himself in our
place, he made it possible for us to have a choice.
We can either remain in sin or allow him to become
our Savior. If we choose for him to be our Savior,
we become, once again, who he created us to be:
righteous and godly, what the Bible calls a peculiar
people. Therefore, even though we have been led
to believe a lie, we can accept Jesus as our deliverer.
Jesus then cleanses us of our sins and makes us look
as if we never did it. Now we are as we once were at

birth. We become reborn and can now take our place in the design of God for our lives. Once again, we have been born to live our lives, free from Satan's lies, as a holy vessel unto the LORD.

I can hear some of you saying, "There is no way someone would choose that lifestyle." I would have. Are there still men becoming priests? Yes. Are there still women becoming nuns? Yes. Are there people who are living celibate lives without Jesus because they don't know who they are? Yes. Don't believe me? You can look them up on the Internet. There is a society living just how I described. If you ask them why, they will tell you they simply have no sexual desire. This tells us that not all eunuchs have been convinced they are homosexual. There are some who are living the nonsexual lifestyle without the understanding of who they are meant to be in Christ.

You will never know what joy, peace, and love washed over me when I discovered that God loved me so much he wanted me for himself. I was able to forgive myself and forgive God for what I thought he had done—creating me a homosexual. I believed the lie and thought he had made me an abomination, with hell as my only future. After all, this is what I had been taught. Do I forgive the church? Yes, I forgive them. How can they teach what they do not understand? As far as their lack of compassion, lack of love, and feeling of alienation, it's not for me to judge. That job belongs to Jesus, the one who created me and has always loved me.

Is There Anything God Can't Do?

There are several things God cannot and will not do. Why? Because he is a holy, righteous, all-knowing, and a forgiving God. He is perfect and the only perfection that will ever exist.

1. God will not hear the prayer of a sinner unless it is an earnest, heartfelt prayer of repentance.

> If I regard iniquity (sin) in my heart, the LORD will not hear me.
>
> Psalm 66:18

2. God cannot make a mistake. He has been in the past, he is in the present, and has walked in the future. He knows all things, what is true, and what shall be.

> I am the Alpha and Omega, the beginning and end, saith the LORD, which is, and which was, and which is to come, the Almighty.
>
> Revelation 1:8

3. God cannot tell a lie. God has so much power that when he speaks whatever he speaks becomes what he says. Therefore, it is impossible for him to lie.

> God is not a man, that he should lie; neither the son of man, that he should repent.
>
> Numbers 23:19

4. God cannot look at sin. He is so righteous he cannot bear to look upon sin.

> Thou art of purer eyes than to behold evil, and canst not look on iniquity.
>
> Habakkuk 1:13

As Jesus hung on the cross, he took our sins upon himself. For this cause, God departed from him and could not look upon him. The Bible says his Father actually turned his back to him as he hung on the cross.

> And at the ninth hour Jesus cried with a loud voice, saying, Eloi, Eloi, la'-ma sa-bach'-tha-ni? Which is, being interpreted, My God, my God, why hast thou forsaken me?
>
> Mark 15:34

5. He cannot remember past sins of which you have repented.

> Saith the LORD: for I will forgive their iniquity, and I will remember their sins no more.
>
> Jeremiah 31:34

> He will turn again, he will have compassion upon us; he will subdue our iniquities; and thou wilt cast all their sins into the depths of the sea.
>
> Micah 7:19

6. God cannot be defeated. He is all-powerful. He is omnipotent.

And I heard as it were the voice of a great multitude, and as the voice of many waters, and as the voice of many thunderings, saying Al-le-lu-ia: for the Lord God omnipotent reigneth.

Revelation 19:6

7. God cannot be out smarted or fooled. The Holy Spirit is God, the Spirit of Truth. He is all-knowing; therefore, it is impossible for him to believe a lie.

Even the Spirit of Truth; whom the world cannot receive, because it seeth him not, neither knoweth him.

John 14:17

Be not deceived; God is not mocked: for whatsoever a man soweth, that shall he also reap.

Galatians 6:7

There is one other thing that God will not do that I have to mention. He will not force himself on anyone. He has given all humanity free will. God created all things; there is nothing in existence that was not created by him.

> For by him were all things created, that are
> in heaven, and that are in earth, visible and
> invisible, whether they be thrones, or domin-
> ions, or principalities, or powers: all things
> were created by him, and for him: And he
> is before all things, and by him all things
> consist.
>
> Colossians 1:16–17

I've heard people ask, "Why didn't he just make a bunch of mini-mes?" If he had done that, there would be no thankfulness, no worship, no praise, and no expression of love. Everyone would be the same. Though our differences are often points of conten-tion, it would be terribly boring without them. There would be no real purpose for our existence. If God created us without free will or without souls, he would have never been able to obtain what he was longing for, which is the same thing he desires today: a relationship with his creation. God wanted a fam-ily; he wanted sons and daughters who would love him because of who he is, not because they had to.

These are some of the things God will not or can not do. There are others, I'm sure. As you can see, he is so holy and righteous, that he is accountable to no one but himself. There is no need for him to be, for this world and everything in it exists on nothing but his Word. If he ever spoke a lie, or did anything unholy, all he has ever spoken into existence would simply cease from being, including you and me.

This is how we know God did not make a mistake; he could not have created anyone to be homosexual and then declare homosexuality to be sin. It is impossible. He said in Genesis 1:26, "Let us make man in our image." What image? The image of righteousness and holiness. This is how he created Adam and Eve and how they existed until their decision to sin. That decision is how and when sin entered the hearts of mankind. Now we are born into sin, which is why even young children are not exempt from the effects of sin.

What Can We Do?

The question shouldn't be, "What can we do?" It should be, "What *must* we do?"

First, we need to stop acting as if the lie that people are born homosexuals doesn't exist. Our kids are now being taught in school that it's okay to have two mommies or two daddies. If you are not careful, they are seeing it on TV. They are being conditioned to accept the lie as truth, without question or consequence.

You have heard the old Shakespearean saying, "He who protest too loudly." Why does the homosexual community protest so loudly? Why do they insist on everyone seeing things the same way they do? There is an emptiness inside them; they are convinced it is because they are not accepted. If they can only have all the rights of a heterosexual, insurance, marriage, families, etc., they believe this emptiness will be filled. If they can get everyone to accept them, they will be justified, made whole, and complete. What they do not understand is everyone, regardless of sexuality, has that same emptiness, hole, or void within them. It is put there by God and can only be filled by God.

Second, we need to take notice of our child's mannerisms and what they are drawn to. We need to start being aware of these things at an early age. I am not saying you should not allow your kids to play with certain toys or stop them from being themselves. I am saying we need to realize our child may be on Satan's hit list. We need to begin to use the weapons God gave us in his Word. We need to start fighting for our children, since they cannot fight for themselves.

What are these weapons?

1. These weapons are only available to Christians since they are given to us by the Holy Spirit of God.

Therefore, you must be a Christian and be filled with the Holy Spirit.

> But ye shall receive power, after that the Holy Ghost is come upon you.
>
> Acts 1:8

2. We must pray and fast. In Mark 9, the disciples were asked to pray for a child. Even though they prayed, the child was not delivered. They asked Jesus why.

> And he said unto them, this kind can come forth by nothing, but by prayer and fasting.
>
> Mark 9:29

This child was not bound by homosexuality; however, the roots of homosexuality run deep. You are not praying for a hangnail. Satan is not going to leave without a tremendous fight. Fasting gets God's attention. He knows, if you are willing to deny yourself, you are seriously wanting and needing his help.

3. You have to put on the whole armor of God.

Be strong in the LORD, and in the power of his might. Put on the whole Armour of God, that ye may be able to stand against the whiles (cunning devices) of the devil.

Ephesians 6:10–11

Stand therefore, having your loins girt about with truth, and having on the breastplate of righteousness; And your feet shod with the preparation of the gospel of peace; Above all, taking the shield of faith, wherewith ye shall be able to quench all the fiery darts of the wicked. And take the helmet of salvation, and the sword of the Spirit, which is the word of God.

Ephesians 6:14–17

I know some of you are feeling overwhelmed, so let's break it down. It's not as hard as it sounds.

Be strong in the LORD, in the power of his might.

Ephesians 6:10

You have to know who your God is. You must realize you are fighting in the power of his might. You must trust him completely and know that there is no greater power, no higher authority, and no greater love than his love for you. He is on your side.

> Stand therefore, having your loins girt about with truth.
>
> Ephesians 6:14

Know the truth. Know who God says you are. Know the Word of God and his promises to each of his children. Example: I can do all things through Christ, who strengthens me. I am the head and not the tail. I am above and not beneath. I am the righteousness of God. I was purchased with a price. I belong to him. He is my strength, my refuge, my high tower, my pleasant help in time of trouble, etc. Know what the Bible says about you and how God sees you.

> Having on the breastplate of righteousness.
>
> Ephesians 6:14

You must know that you are in right standing with God. You are covered by the blood of Jesus and grafted into his family; you are his child, and he is your father. There is nothing that can separate you from him. He lives within you, and you live within him. He has you covered. You have been given authority, through salvation, to enter into the throne room of God and declare the name of Jesus as your rite of passage.

> Have your feet shod with the preparation of the gospel.
>
> Ephesians 6:15

The Bible says that your steps are ordered by the LORD. He knows where you are, and he has fitted you with his Word, the gospel of peace.

> Above all, taking the shield of faith.
>
> Ephesians 6:16

Without faith, it is impossible to please God. Without faith, we cannot call God "Father" or Jesus "LORD." There is nothing too hard for God.

> So then faith cometh by hearing, and hearing by the word of God.
>
> Romans 10:17

> For by grace are ye saved through faith; and that not of yourselves; it is the gift of God.
>
> Ephesians 2:8

VANESSA HEADRICK

The ability to believe in what we have not seen is a gift of God. The more we hear or read the Word, the more our faith grows. It is our inextinguishable hope of glory. The Bible says everyone is given a measure of faith; however, we do not have to settle for that measure. We can cause that measure to grow by filling our minds and spirit with the Word of God, which increases our faith.

God plants the seed of faith within us. It is up to us to water and nourish that seed by reading God's Word, singing praises, hearing sermons or teachings, praying, and studying. The more we learn, the larger our faith grows, along with our love of God. By doing these things, we are able to believe or have faith in things that at one time seemed impossible. You have to be able to believe, without doubting, that God is willing and able to accomplish what you are believing for.

Take the helmet of salvation.

Ephesians 6:17

The helmet of salvation covers your mind. The battle can be won or lost, depending on your mind. Do you see the glass half empty or half full? You must determine in your mind that you will not give up, regardless of what you see.

> They that observe lying vanities forsake their
> own mercy.
>
> Jonah 2:8

You can see, in this verse, that what you see and what you perceive to be truth are often strategically planted lies, presented by Satan, to convince you that you've already lost the battle. It is not true; it is simply a weapon Satan uses against you. You cannot allow yourself to be moved by what you see. You have to be convinced, in your spirit and your mind, that God's Word cannot fail.

> And let us not be weary in well doing: for in
> due season we shall reap, if we faint not.
>
> Galatians 6:9

You have to refuse to give up. Many times, things look worse right before your breakthrough, right before the battle is won. The Bible says when you have done all you know to do, stand, dig your heels in, and refuse to be moved. Get a pit-bull spirit, sink your teeth in, and refuse to let go until God shows up and defeats Satan on your behalf.

I questioned whether to tell the following story or not, but it is the truth and shows how what I am telling you works. Years ago, I had to fight my own demons in order to be totally delivered from the spirit of homosexuality. Each night, as I tried to go to sleep, I would be attacked by demons. Night after night, they would come and refuse to allow me any rest or peace. Finally, after weeks of this, I made up my mind that enough was enough.

The night began as usual. I lay down, almost got to sleep, and here they came. I fought them for as long as I thought I could. I got up to go to another room. As I started toward the door, Ephesians 6:13 came into my spirit.

> Wherefore take unto you the whole Armour
> of God, that ye may be able to withstand in
> the evil day, and having done all, to stand.
> Stand therefore,
>
> Ephesians 6:13

I took my stand and refused to be moved. I had always been taught that at the name of Jesus, demons had to flee. So with all the authority I could muster,

I said, "In the name of Jesus, I command you to go." To my horror, they chimed back at me, in unison, "In the name of Jesus." For a second, I felt totally defeated, as if the wind had been knocked out of me.

If I had believed the lying vanity of which I was seeing, I would have been defeated. All of a sudden, I heard the Holy Spirit say, "It's in the blood." What's in the blood? Power. I took my stand and declared, "I plead the blood of Jesus"; before I could finish what I was going to say, they were instantly gone.

Where was this battle won? In my mind. Where could it have been lost? In my mind. Our minds are an extremely powerful weapon. When loaded with the right ammunition, it will leave the enemy defenseless.

> The sword of the Spirit, which is the word of God.
>
> Ephesians 6:17

The sword of the Spirit is our only defensive weapon. The rest is all armor. It is the only defensive weapon needed. There is nothing more powerful than the Word of God. In the story I just told you, you can see how I had to make a decision to stand in my mind, but it was the Word that I spoke, the Word I believed and had faith in, that actually won the battle. God's Word cannot fail.

Third, and most important, we have to start teaching our children the truth. There are three kinds of lifestyles. Two will get you to heaven, if lived as a Christian. One will take you to hell.

- Lifestyle #1: Heterosexual
- Lifestyle #2: Homosexual
- Lifestyle #3: Nonsexual

Some of you are thinking that this is too extreme. Satan is taking extreme measures; therefore, we have to also. The Bible is filled with people who God used to do tremendous things; yet, they were all required to take extreme measures, leaps of faith, in order to accomplish them.

For those of you who do not want your children to know about homosexuality, you are not living in reality. They are being taught. Don't you think you should be the one doing the teaching? After all, you are the only one who will tell them the truth. They need to be taught that God created some people for himself. It's okay not to get married or have children. It's okay to live life dedicated to God, to be used as a missionary, preacher, teacher, or prophet. It's okay to live life nonsexual, holy, and blessed by the LORD.

Preachers, you have got to stop telling homosexuals that they are an abomination with contempt and disdain in your voice. I understand that tone is there because of your hatred for the sin, but they do not understand that. It comes across as you hate them, which I know you do not. Instead, tell them that God loves them. Tell them who they really are. Tell them that God created them different for a purpose—his own purpose. It is your job, Christians, to pick them up out of the rubbish and begin to polish away the hatred, fear, loneliness, and inability to forgive. Love them into the kingdom, and let's place them back on the wall.

> Even unto them (eunuchs) will I give in mine house and within my walls a place.
>
> Isaiah 56:5

STRONGHOLDS

The word *stronghold* often brings to mind forts or castles surrounded by moats and guards, a place meant to be impassable and safe. However, the strongholds I want to talk about are in our minds. They are traps set up by Satan to ensnare and control his prey: mankind.

> Be sober, be vigilant; because your adversary the devil, as a roaring lion, walketh about, seeking whom he may devour:
>
> 1 Peter 5:8

I love to fish, and my favorite fish to catch is a catfish. A catfish usually does not hit the bait and make a run for it, like a bass. A catfish nibbles at the bait for a while as if to see if he wants it or not. When you least expect it, he will finally grab a hold of it; still, you will miss him if you do not set the hook. Once the hook is set, you've got him.

This is how Satan ensnares us. He places bait in front of us. For Eve, it was the forbidden fruit. I'm sure Eve had passed the fruit many times. One day, it caught her eye. She thought to herself, *I wonder what that tastes like.* She pushed the thought out of her mind and kept walking.

The next day, she passed by, saw the fruit, stopped, and looked at it. She didn't push the thought out of her mind so quickly. She stood there, looking. She thought, *There is so much fruit; no one will notice if I take some.* She remembered God's warning: if you eat of this tree, you will surely die. Suddenly, she snapped back to reality and walked on by.

The next day, she stopped, reached out, and touched it. She heard no voice from heaven, heard no thunder, and saw no lightning bolts. She thought about how pretty and colorful the fruit was and how smooth and cool it felt in her hand. Just then, she heard Adam calling her. So again, she walked on by, leaving the fruit hanging on the tree. The temptation began to consume her thoughts. She would be nowhere near the tree and find herself thinking about it. Her ability to push the thoughts out of her mind became harder and harder.

Finally, she couldn't stand it any longer. She didn't just pass by the tree; she willingly went to the tree. She reached out, took a piece, and ate it. This is exactly how the devil entraps us: with temptation. It is up to us to push the thoughts out of our minds. You can only do this on purpose. You have to intentionally take control of what you are thinking and replace it with something else.

Eve was immediately filled with guilt when she ate the fruit. There is something in us as humans; we do not want to bear our guilt alone. If someone else is guilty of the same things, we somehow feel vindicated. So Eve took the fruit to Adam. Adam, seeing that Eve looked the same and certainly wasn't dead, took the piece of fruit, and he too ate. Satan dangled the bait in front of them. Eve, through her temptation, had nibbled at it; finally, just like the catfish, she grabbed it. In sharing it with Adam, the hook was set.

Did they die in the flesh? No. There was, however, a death in their spirit. No longer could they stand guiltless before God. Satan now had a hold on them. They would never be the same again. As punishment, Adam had to work for their food. Eve would have to bear pain in childbirth. They were thrown out of the Garden of Eden. The stronghold of sin now had control of them. Because of their failure, we are still living in sin today.

Sin will always cost you something. For the prostitute, it is her self-worth and self-esteem; for the alcoholic and drug addict, it is their pride, their relationships, and their families; for the homosexual, it is what could have been.

It cost Adam and Eve the life of their son, Abel. If it had not been for the sin that they were responsible for, their son Cain would not have murdered Abel, their other son. You see, Satan does not practice catch and release like I do when I am fishing. The only release you will ever find for your sins is Jesus. He is the only way for someone bound by a stronghold to be set free. He paid the price on the cross. By dying on the cross, he purchased us back from the devil, whom we gave ourselves to by sinning. His death made a way for you and I to be free from what once had us bound.

Is all sin a stronghold? No. But all sin has the potential of becoming one. If you allow a sin to grow and begin to dictate and control you, or if you are hooked and no longer have a choice, it has you. If the addiction or action is stronger than your will, it is a stronghold.

This is how we know homosexuality cannot be helped. The person has no choice and can never be totally free without Jesus. He is the only one who has the key to unlock what has them held captive. This is not, however, automatic; they have to go to him, be willing to give up what holds them, and ask him to set them free. This is where the problem lies. Some people like their bondage.

Most people are born, grow up, and then, somewhere in their lives, they are introduced to whatever binds them. The drug addict, the alcoholic, and the pornographer—they all had a life before their sin. They can remember what it was like before they became addicted. You can ask the alcoholic if he is an alcoholic, and unless he has hit bottom and had to face the truth, he will say no. These people do not want to own their sin. They know they have a problem. They do not believe, however, that they are the problem.

The homosexual is so convinced that he or she was born that way, because they cannot remember life before. They cannot look back on their lives and remember themselves any other way. Therefore, they must have been born that way, which makes them their sin. It is their identity. It is who they truly believe they are.

I'll never forget when I brought someone home with me to eat dinner at my mom's. I had brought people home before. This time, I could tell my mom was really upset. Later, I asked her what was wrong. She began to cry and said this friend upset her so badly because she looked like a homosexual. At first, I didn't understand her reaction. My mom knew of my lifestyle; she knew I was with these other people. But this time, she couldn't deny it or act like it wasn't true. It was there and sitting at her dinner table.

You see, I never stopped to consider anyone's feelings but my own. At that time, I liked my bondage. I was having a good time and didn't care who knew it, who liked it, or who didn't like it. After all, I was just being me, or so I thought.

Regardless of my attitude, my mother never gave up on me. I will never know how many prayers my mom has prayed or how many tears she has shed. I do not know how many nights she has lain awake, not knowing where I was or if I was okay. I do know how she refused to give up and the choice she made to love me more than she hated the sin.

I'm sure some of you reading this cannot understand how a praying, Christian woman, would allow me to bring these people into her home. Simple: I was these people. She realized if I was her baby, these people were someone's baby too.

After she got over the shock of how my girlfriend looked, I remember she said she was trying to pray for me, when the LORD told her she had to pray for my girlfriend too. He wasn't going to allow her to pray for me without praying for her soul also. I can't imagine how hard that was for her. In order to earnestly pray for her, it meant she had to accept and love her.

My mom refused to accept my lifestyle or my attitude. She believed prayer was the answer and that it would change me even if I did not want to be changed. She prayed for my girlfriend and me for ten years without fail. She stood in the gap for us and refused to be denied. Finally, her prayers were answered. God saved us both, filled us both with his Holy Spirit, and changed us both. As far as I know, we are both free today, I believe because of her love and faithfulness.

Never give up on your loved one. It doesn't matter if they like their bondage or not. Hold them up before the LORD, and continue to believe. God can do the impossible.

Do We Really Believe?

Do we, as Christians and ministers, really believe what we confess? Do we really believe the blood of Jesus has the power to wash and cleanse every sin? I was raised to believe this to be true. Imagine my surprise when I became a Christian and how no one around me seemed to believe what they had taught me. I expected my family and church to celebrate my rebirth. I thought they would accept me with open arms as a new creation.

> Therefore if any man be in Christ, he is a new creature; old things are passed away; behold, all things are become new.
>
> 2 Corinthians 5:17

I had heard this verse quoted and preached my entire life. It is one of those scriptures that is repeated so often it seems to lose it's meaning.

Instead of being accepted as a blood-bought child of God, I was still viewed as a homosexual. It didn't seem to matter how much I changed, how much I studied, how much I exhibited the fruits of the Spirit in my life. I was refused forgiveness and acceptance in the church.

I've always heard an elephant never forgets; unfortunately, neither do some Christians. Don't get me wrong, there are ministers and Christians who really do show the love of God; they really do accept and believe God's ability to save and change a sinner into his likeness. This, however, was not my experience. I needed to be recognized. I needed to be mentored. I needed an elder's wisdom, anointing, and influence to be deposited into my spirit. Because of my past, I was denied these invaluable relationships. Although I have been saved and filled with the Holy Spirit for many years, I still have not found a church that will accept me. When I first got saved, this really bothered and hurt me; however, I made up my mind I would not be denied.

My cousin loaned me a book by Benny Hinn called *Good Morning, Holy Spirit*. I knew God was no respecter of persons. I believed what the Holy Spirit had done for Benny, he would do for me. I earnestly asked the Holy Spirit to teach me and become my friend. He was faithful and began to give me revelations into the mysteries written in the Word of God. What better teacher can anyone ask for than the Holy Spirit himself?

In some ways, my journey has been harder because of these relationships I am being denied. It's important to be accountable to someone.

> Two are better than one; because they have a good reward for their labor. For if they fall, the one will lift up his fellow: but woe to him that is alone when he falleth; for he hath not another to help him up.
>
> Ecclesiastes 4:9–10

Why am I telling you this? I want you to understand that anyone, regardless of their past, can be called of God. God believes his word and is faithful to keep it. I can tell you, if I had not have come from a Christian family, if I had not of had the encounters with the LORD I have had, I would have given up and gone back to homosexuality because of the experiences I have had with the church.

If you are a Christian or a minister, please allow God to give you the ability to release people from their pasts. Release them from their sins. Allow God to make of them whatever he chooses.

> Judge not, that ye be not judged. For with what judgment ye judge, ye shall be judged: and with what measure ye mete, it shall be measured to you again.
>
> Matthew 7:1–2

I'm sure almost everyone knows or has heard these verses; yet, we apparently do not believe Jesus knew what he was talking about. If Jesus can forgive us of whatever we have done that caused him to be crucified, what gives anyone the right to hold others without forgiveness? We refuse to forgive people for things they didn't even do to us. Isn't that insane? Let's get back to believing God's Word.

> For if we forgive men their trespasses, your heavenly Father will also forgive you: But if ye forgive not men their trespasses, neither will your Father forgive your trespasses.
>
> Matthew 6:14–15

We are all guilty of something. We all have a past. In Corinthians, Paul is talking to the saints and has need to remind them of their imperfections.

> Know ye not that the unrighteous shall not inherit the kingdom of God? Be not deceived: neither fornicators, nor idolaters, nor adulterers, nor effeminate, nor abusers of themselves with mankind, nor thieves, nor covetous, nor drunkards, nor revilers, nor extortioners, shall inherit the kingdom of God.
>
> 1 Corinthians 6:9–10

Take note: homosexuals are included in this list. It is verse 11, however I want you to read and think on.

> And such were some of you: but ye are washed, but ye are sanctified, but ye are justified in the name of the LORD Jesus, and by the Spirit of God.
>
> 1 Corinthians 6:11

It does not matter what kind of sinner you were, including homosexuality; when God forgives you, he released you from your past. If God did this for you, don't you think he expects you to do the same? It may surprise you what God will do with them, how he may use them, and how, one day, they may be a blessing to you, your church, or family. In order for this to happen, you have got to give them a chance. You have to show them brotherly love and help them to grow into their purpose.

Don't Get Stuck

The Bible says that God does not change. While it is true that God's Word, his mercy, his grace, and his personality, do not change, the way in which God accomplishes his will does. One reason Jesus came to this earth was not only to provide a way for us to be forgiven and grafted into the family of God but was to introduce a new way of thinking and a new insight into the personality of God. This new idea, this new way of living, is called *grace*.

In the *New Strong's Exhaustive Concordance*, grace[1] is defined in two parts.

1. *Greek*: an impassable internal, gulf.

Greek: graciousness, of manner or act, divine influence upon the heart and its reflection in the life, acceptable, favor, gift, liberality.

In the first definition, we see a place of separation, an impassable, unapproachable gulf, which denied anyone a personal relationship with God. This is how believers lived at the time Jesus began his ministry. Only the priest was allowed into his presence. If the priest had any iniquity found in him, God would strike him dead.

Jesus came to remove this gulf, this gap, between God and his people. Jesus had such a hard time delivering his message of grace—the second definition: a gift of favor, liberty, and mercy—because it meant the people had to accept the fact that God was doing something new. Though that has been over two thousand years ago, it is interesting to see that people are still the same. We still have problems accepting when God wants to do something new. We want to keep God in a box—a box of comfort, tradition, belief, and doctrine.

Jesus didn't, however, have as much resistance from the people as he did the religious leaders of the time. The message he was delivering to the people brought them hope, freedom, and love. The leaders, the scribes and Pharisees, saw this new message as a threat. Their power and control over the people was being challenged, which is why they wanted to kill him.

There are still people like the scribes and Pharisees today. They are bound in religion and old traditions. They are afraid of accepting anything new; they too are scared of losing control. It doesn't take a brain surgeon to understand if something is no longer working, we must change that something.

Several years ago, TBN made their first movie, *China Cry*. Several members of my family and I decided to go see it. It was a Saturday night; we all met, went out to eat, went to see the movie, and had a terrific time together. The next morning, at church, the preacher got up and preached how going to the theater, even to see this movie, was a sin. Why couldn't he see God was doing something new? Why couldn't he see that if God was in it, which he was, that it was our place, as his children, to support it? The answer to both of these questions is simple: he was stuck.

He was stuck in religion, tradition, and doctrine. He was stuck in a thought process that was decades old. We have to acknowledge God has given people ideas and inventions for a reason. Whether they are a sinner or a saint, God gave them their talents. If there is any way we as Christians can use them for the furtherance of the gospel, I believe we are obligated to do so, which includes going into perceived sinner territory. To do anything less is letting God down in our commission to cover the world with the his Word.

People who need to know God the worst are not in the church house. A few years ago, I was sitting in my car. I was getting ready to go into the church. As I was sitting there, looking at the building, the Holy Spirit spoke a word into my spirit. He said, "Those walls are not there to keep the people inside safe; they are there to keep sinners safely on the outside." The words I heard stung in my spirit, but I had to admit their truth. We are never going to reach the world from inside a church. We have to come out from behind our walls of safety. We have to use every means available to reach a hurting, dying world. We have to stop allowing the devil to intimidate us and blind us to the possibilities that are available to the church.

Don't get stuck. Let's not be like the scribes and Pharisees. Let's open our eyes and our hearts and allow God to use us in any available way possible. We have got to be more like Jesus and spread the word of grace, even when we are met by the twin spirits of religion and tradition.

You may be wondering what getting stuck has to do with homosexuality. It is from these twin spirits that people become bound and set in their ways of thinking. It is because of religion and tradition that people think they know better than God, who is worthy of forgiveness, and whom God will or will not use. I have been told, more than once, by pastors that I would never be allowed to do anything in their church. I think they have forgotten whose church it really is. The church belongs to God.

I am challenging these spirits of control by writing this book. The sermon (Sodom and Gomorrah), which I have dissected, has been preached repeatedly for many years. In fact, I heard it on television the very day I wrote this chapter. In order for this new message, this plea for mercy and understanding for the souls of the homosexual, the revelation of the nonsexual lifestyle, and the importance of who God created these people to be, will only come about through a move of the Holy Spirit and the church's willingness to allow him to change their minds and hearts.

If the church remains stuck, this field will largely go unharvested, millions x multiplied thousands of souls will go to hell without ever knowing the truth of who they were meant to be. They will never know that God had a special place in his heart for them, a special blessing awaiting them, for living a sacrificial life of loss here on earth for a greater gain in heaven. They will die believing the lie that God created them for destruction.

I do not believe there is one word in the Bible put there by coincidence or without purpose. Every detail is for revelation and insight. In 2 Kings 9:30-37, we read of the death of Jezebel. She was the high priestess of Baal. They worshiped demons of sexual perversion, greed, violence, and child sacrifice.

These are the same spirits alive and well today. Greed is seen everyday. It is what has caused this nation to be on the edge of financial ruin. Violence is out of control. Crimes of rape, murder, and gang activity are in every state, city, and town. Child sacrifice is at an all time high—everything from parental homicide to abortion. There are literally thousands of children killed daily. Then we have sexual perversion. Anything that has entered the imagination is being done, most too vial to speak of, including sexual slavery of not just women, but children as young as three-years-old have been reported. Then, of course, I must add adultery, fornication, and homosexuality.

> If a house be divided against itself, that house cannot stand.
>
> Mark 3:25

In this verse, Jesus is telling us the best way to destroy something is from the inside. I saw part of a television show that was telling how they destroy a building using dynamite. The man explained that you never place the dynamite on the outside; even though it may do great damage, it will not totally bring the building down. You have to strategically place the dynamite throughout the inside, which will cause it to implode instead of explode. If it explodes from the outside, much of the blast is ineffective. If it implodes, the blast is contained, causing the building to completely be destroyed.

Julius Ceaser was killed by those close enough to repeatedly stick a dagger into him, by those he trusted, by men on the inside. Jesus was betrayed with a kiss from Judas. He was one of his disciples, someone on the inside. Jezebel was destroyed by those on the inside of the castle with her.

> 32 And he lifted up his face to the window, and said, Who is on my side? Who? And there looked out to him two or three eunuchs.
>
> 33 And he said, Throw her down. So they threw her down: and some of her blood was sprinkled on the wall, and on the horses: and he trode her under foot.
>
> 2 Kings 9:32-33

Who did God use to destroy the high priestess of sexual perversion? People on the inside, in this case eunuchs. I do not believe this is recorded in God's Word by chance. It is his way of telling us the only way to destroy the lie of homosexuality is for those on the inside seeing their way out. These eunuchs looked out the window and were filled with an expectation of a new life. They suddenly saw possibility—seeing someone already free, already on the outside, teaching, preaching, declaring, and proclaiming to them their true potential, their way to freedom, their purpose and destiny.

In order for the homosexual to ever hear this message, the church has to break free from being stuck in religion and traditions. We have to begin to use all means available to deliver this new revelation. By doing this, we can begin to cause homosexuality to implode by reaching those on the inside and bringing them out. This will cause the division to become greater and greater until Satan's lie spiritually implodes.

> And if Satan rise up against himself, and be divided, he cannot stand, but hath and end.
>
> Mark 3:26

CAN LOVE
BUILD A BRIDGE?

I know I have come down hard on the church. Don't get me wrong. Try to understand the spirit in which this criticism is given. I love the church and the ministers that God has called to preach his Word. All I am asking is, if you don't understand something, don't regurgitate what you have heard someone else say who didn't understand either. Realize what has been preached for decades is not working. It is not working because it is not the heart of God. We have to admit when we are wrong and be willing to hear and understand the truth when we hear it, even when it is not easy to accept. If a message is not reaching the people it is intended for, there has to be something wrong with the message.

God's Word is truth. His Word heals and sets the captives free. In this case, the captives are still being held captive. Has God's Word failed, or have we as the church failed in the interpretation of the Word? We both know the answer to that question.

Time is short. We can all agree the world cannot go on much longer in the direction it is going. I believe Jesus has his hand on the door of heaven, getting ready to swing it open to come and receive his bride. We, as his church, cannot allow this to happen without an earnest, compassionate, truthful, attempt to harvest the fields of homosexuality.

These people have not gone too far that the hand of God cannot reach them. God's heart has not been hardened to where he does not love them. He loves them as much today as the day he created them. They were not created for the day of destruction, which I have also heard preached. They were created with gifts and talents, created as prophets, evangelists, pastors, teachers, writers, and praise and worship leaders; they were created to serve God.

Please help me to begin to build a bridge over the gulf of misunderstanding, rejection, half-truths, alienation, pride, prejudice, and mistrust that separates the homosexual from the church and the church from the homosexual. It is not the homosexual's place to reach out to the church; it is the churches place, as representatives of Christ, to reach out to them. We need to apologize for our hardness and indifference. We need to let them know they are welcome in the house of God and that they will be met with love and compassion.

Loving the person trapped in the bondage of sin does not mean we are condoning their lifestyle. The roots of my family run deep in the Pentecostal Church of God, yet they always stood by me and loved me. Never did I get their love for me confused and think it meant they accepted my lifestyle. They hated the sin but loved me unconditionally. They fasted and prayed for over twenty years for my soul. They refused to give up. There are other families out there, right now, who are doing the same for their loved one; many are afraid to let the church know and afraid to take off the happy face masks. They are scared they may be judged or alienated for not having the perfect family.

The Bible says we are to agree in prayer. To agree in prayer for these loved ones means you too would have to love them. You cannot earnestly pray for someone without love, compassion, and, in this case, empathy for their family. If you do not have this for the homosexual community, please ask the LORD to give you a heart for them. I have faith that he will do just that.

If your family has not been touched by this sin, it is only because of the grace of God. It doesn't matter who you are. You can be a pastor, bishop, missionary, or Sunday school teacher. Satan is not prejudiced. It may, one day, be your child or grandchild who needs prayer.

> Again I say unto you, That if two of you shall agree on earth as touching any thing that they shall ask, it shall be done for them of my Father, which is in heaven.
>
> Matthew 18:19

LET MY PEOPLE GO

I am reminded of the Israelite people, who were held in bondage as slaves. They had been enslaved for over four hundred years. They were created and chosen by God to be his people. They, however, were held in bondage so long they began to forget who they were. They still told the stories of what God had done for them in the past, but they were becoming just that: stories.

They were held in Egypt by a king who believed himself to be God. The same is true today. Satan believes himself to be God. He is, however, the god over sin and sinners. He is not all-powerful or all-knowing; he is limited by the true and living God of all, LORD God Jehovah.

Moses was raised in the king's castle. He was taught all the ways of the Egyptians. He was brought up as a son of Pharaoh. He had everything anyone of that time could possibly want. He ate the best foods, wore the best clothes, and was highly educated—he was royalty. The problem was, he was not Egyptian; he was Israeli.

For those who do not know the story, I will quickly tell you. If you have a Bible, you can read this story in Exodus 1.

Though the children of Israel were slaves, they began to grow in number to the point Pharaoh began to see them as a threat. He was afraid that if they decided to go to war against the Egyptians, they would be outnumbered. Pharaoh instructed the midwives to kill all male children at the time of their births. The midwives feared God and allowed the children to live. God rewarded the midwives by giving them families of their own.

Pharaoh decided that since that didn't work, he would instruct his people to throw all Israeli boys into the river. Moses's mother took Moses, put him in the river in a pitched-lined basket, trusting God to save him. Pharaoh's daughter found him and took him as her own son. Moses was adopted into Pharaoh's family.

When Moses grew up, he couldn't stand to see his people suffering. One day, he saw an Egyptian beating one of the slaves. Moses killed the Egyptian and saved the life of the slave. When Pharaoh heard what he had done, he sought to kill him. Moses fled into the land of Midian, where he married and tended sheep. It was at that time God called Moses from a burning bush, instructing him to go back to Egypt and lead the children of Israel to freedom.

Now that we all know the story, let me explain to you why I am reminded of it. I feel a little like Moses must have felt when he saw the Egyptian mistreating the slave. Being raised in a godly family, I was taught and educated in the Word of God. I left this environment and spent years living in a type of *Midian*[1], which in the Hebrew means "a place of discord and strife." Strife[2] means "a place of controversy or debate." This is where I lived for many years: in a constant state of internal debate and controversy; a debate between what I knew was truth, the Word of God, and the lie of which I was convinced was also true.

Since then, I have been set free from this controversy, this lie, and this bondage. I am, however, seeing my passion, my people suffering wrongs. They are not only suffering wrong by Satan and people who are prejudice, they are being wronged by some of God's representatives. I feel it is my call, my assignment, to lift up my voice and demand, "Let my people go."

Picture, if you will, what I see in my spirit. These people, my people, are armed with the knowledge of truth. The knowledge of how Satan has kept them in bondage for their entire lives. The truth of how God had created them to be a blessing unto himself. Million x multiplied thousands of people, filled with the spirit of God, rising up in holy anger against the one who has enslaved them.

What a powerful army they would be. Satan, unknowingly, has already armed them with some important qualities needed to be radical Christians. They do not care what others think of them. They don't care if their beliefs are not eagerly accepted. They are accustomed to people talking about them and whispering behind their backs. They are willing to stand up for what they believe, regardless of the costs. An army like this would definitely be a holy nightmare for Satan.

Am I dreaming? Yes, but I believe my God can make dreams come true. I believe what the Bible says.

> With men it is impossible, but not with God:
> for with God all things are possible.
>
> Mark 10:27

It is impossible for a sea to part for thousands to pass through on dry ground. It is impossible to be thrown into a furnace and come out without even the smell of smoke on you. It is impossible for a man to reach out, lean on two pillars, and cause an entire coliseum to collapse. All of these things are impossible, except for an all-knowing, all-powerful God. With my God, my dreams are possible.

It is time for the lie of which Satan has convinced them is true to be nullified by the real truth. It is time for Satan to let them go to sacrifice unto the LORD. It is time he let them go on a journey to find their promised land. A place where they are free from bondage, free from the internal strife, free to receive from God what belongs to them. It's time they are told the truth about who they are and receive forgiveness, peace, joy, and love. It's time that we, as the church, refuse to sit passably by and allow them to remain enslaved to a lesser god—the god of this world, Satan. It's time we lead them to the God of truth. For it is the truth that will make them free—free *indeed.*

> If the Son therefore shall make you free, ye shall be free indeed.
>
> John 8:36

> Jesus saith unto him, I am the way, the truth, and the life: no man cometh unto the Father, but by me.
>
> John 14:6

In Acts 1:4, Jesus told his disciples to wait in Jerusalem until they had received the promise of the Father—the *indeed.*

> And, behold, I send the promise of my Father upon you: but tarry ye in the city of Jerusalem, until ye be endued with power from on high.
>
> Luke 24:49

You see, it is possible to be a Christian and be forgiven for your sins but still not have the power needed to overcome that which holds you bound. It is the indeed that will destroy the curse and give you the ability to be set free from the spirit of homosexuality. Without the indeed, you will still be in a constant battle in your mind, body, and spirit, though your soul is free from sin. We know, whether we understand it or not, that the spirit of homosexuality is powerful and all consuming. However, it cannot stand when placed under the power of the Holy Spirit; it must relinquish its territory and admit defeat. It must bow its knee.

Jesus knew it would be impossible for his disciples and his followers to complete the Great Commission without the power of which he possessed. Jesus commissioned us in his last statement before his ascension into glory.

> And he said unto them, Go ye into all the world, and preach the gospel to every creature. He that believeth and is baptized shall be saved; but he that believeth not shall be damned. And these signs shall follow them that believe; In my name shall they cast out devils; they shall speak with new tongues; They shall take up serpents; and if they drink

any deadly thing, it shall not hurt them; they shall lay hands on the sick, and they shall recover.

Mark 16:15–18

Jesus knew there was no way for his followers to follow his instructions without the promise of the Father. He knew there was no way we could defeat the devil without his supernatural power from on high.

It is impossible for anyone to become totally free unless the power of the Holy Spirit is residing within them. So for those who say they are now straight and living a life of heterosexuality but deny and refuse the entrance of the Holy Spirit, they are deceived. They will fail because the root, the curse, and spirits that bind them have not and cannot be removed without the supernatural strength given only by the Holy Spirit. They must have the opportunity and teaching that will lead them to this truth which they will not receive if not welcomed and loved by the body of Christ.

By the church being unwilling to reach out in love and without judgment to the homosexual, they are, in part, refusing to obey the Great Commission of Jesus. They are withholding the knowledge and power that the homosexual must have to ever become what God created them to be. We, as the church, must understand the day in which we live and take the authority we have been given by the Holy Spirit and allow him, through us, to set the captive free. It is the only hope and the only way the fields of homosexuality will be harvested and my people will be set free. If the church refuses to reach out, the homosexual will never be able to take their place back on the wall and accomplish their destiny and their calling of which God created them to fulfill.

The Bible says there is a time and a season for all things. The children of Israel were held in bondage for over four hundred years, but the time came, the appointed time, that God had predetermined and established for their deliverance. I believe the time, the appointed time, has come for the church to be educated and brought to understanding and knowledge on how to successfully minister to the homosexual. The time has come for their deliverance. It is time to let my people go.

The church has to learn what they have been doing wrong. They have to accept the fact that there are things they do not understand. They must allow love to motivate them into areas of which they may not be comfortable and allow the LORD to use people they may not have chosen to teach them what they need to know on how to reach those who, at one time, were thought to be unreachable. They must be willing to allow the Holy Spirit to speak truth into them that they may not want to hear. This is how we grow into the likeness of our LORD: by allowing the Holy Spirit to create love in us where at one time was confusion and even fear.

> But these speak evil of those thing which they know not: but what they know naturally, as brute beasts, in those things they corrupt themselves.
>
> Jude 1:10

In this verse, it says to the ministers and teachers, *If you do not understand something, you are not supposed to even try to teach or preach it.* He says, *If you do, it will come across as brutish; you will be ministering from your flesh and not from the heart of God.* I believe this is why the words spoken in the name of Jesus are further hardening the hearts of the homosexual. We have men and women of God feeling like they should say something against the sin, especially since the marriage debate has begun, but they do not have understanding, neither has the Holy Spirit given them knowledge on the subject. I truly believe this is the time and why God has called me to give understanding and insight to his ministers and teachers.

This so-called sermon heard repeatedly—using Sodom and Gomorrah; God created Adam and Eve, not Adam and Steve; it is a life they have chosen; and they are an abomination, is doing more harm than good. It is being preached by people who have limited understanding. The Bible says they should not be preaching on this subject for this reason. They are speaking to people who do not speak the same language. Those of us who have been raised in the church understand the church lingo. We know when a preacher calls a sin an "abomination" that they are talking about the sin and not the person committing the sin. The world, however, does not understand the difference. What they hear is that you just called them an abomination. There is a big difference in what is being said and what is being heard. We must keep this in mind.

I'll give you and example. When my cousin was about four years old, she was extremely thin, all arms and legs. She had brown hair and brown eyes. There was something about her appearance that reminded me of a baby monkey. I began to call her "Monkey," as a nickname. I did not, in any way, mean for this to hurt her or make her feel less than the rest of us. One day, while we were all in the backyard, we were singing, "Jesus Loves the Little Children." She stopped, looked at us, and asked us, "Does God love monkeys too?" It was not a pleasant wake-up call for me. I realized what I meant by calling her monkey was not what she was hearing or understanding.

When ministers tell the homosexual they are an abomination and that they chose their lifestyle, the homosexual is hearing this: you were created for hell, there is nothing you can do about it, and I am completely ignorant on this subject. I think we can agree that this is not the message we are trying to convey. Yet, it is what we are saying, in their language. This is exactly what Jude was trying to keep from happening. We, however, continue to do it, not understanding what we are actually saying. We are, in effect, telling them that there is nothing that can be done for them and they might as well live their lives any way they choose, since their destiny is hell. The Word of God is never meant to condemn the sinner without giving them the good news—the news that he is the answer, he understands their situation, and has conquered the problem, regardless what it is.

Now, if you are truly a man or woman of God, I know this is hard for you to accept. We are supposed to have heavy hearts for unsaved souls. However, we must realize how we have added injury to these already-injured people. This realization should break our hearts and hopefully change the way the church views the homosexual. Instead of the preacher making negative remarks toward them and the whole church clapping and shouting in agreement, maybe we, as a unified body, can hold them up in prayers of true mercy and compassion.

I am sorry to have to bring you to this realization; however, if I did nothing, I would be the one responsible. The more you understand, the more knowledge acquired, the more you are accountable for. I believe the reason God allowed homosexuality in my life is to teach and alert those who have no experience in this area. You can never have real understanding into someone's life, unless you have lived the same life. You can't hear as the world hears, unless you have lived there. Thank God I no longer live there, but I still know the language. I consider it an honor to be able to translate for the glory of God.

It's Not Too Late

If you, or someone you love, are a homosexual, it's not too late.

> Therefore if any man be in Christ, he is a new creature, old things are passed away; behold, all things are become new.
>
> 2 Corinthians 5:17

> I, even I, am he that blotteth out thy transgressions for mine own sake, and will not remember thy sins.
>
> Isaiah 43:25

God has the ability to do what we, as humans, cannot: forget. Once you have asked forgiveness for something you've done from a sincere heart, God forgets it. If you bring it up, he doesn't even know what you are talking about. He doesn't just forgive; he completely forgets, never to be remembered against you again. Isn't that great?

Did you know there is a wonderful promise given, especially to eunuchs, by God? It can be yours.

> For thus saith the LORD unto the eunuchs that keep my sabbaths, and choose the things that please me, and take hold of my covenant (promise). Even unto them will I give in mine house and within my walls a place and a name better than of sons and of daughters: I will give them an everlasting name, that shall not be cut off.
>
> Isaiah 56:4–5

That is an amazing promise. The sons and daughters he is talking about are the Israeli people, who accept him as LORD. They are his chosen people; yet, he says you can receive a place better than them. If I had heard this and not read it in the Bible for myself, I probably would not believe it; yet, there it is. This must mean he really loves us and shows us how seriously he takes our purpose, our calling.

Satan knows you were created specifically for God. He knows this because he too had a special place in heaven. He was created an archangel, the most beautiful angel ever created. He allowed pride and jealousy to enter into his heart. Therefore, he was cast out of heaven. He lost his place, his standing before God. He now is consumed with jealousy for you because he knows you can do something he can never do: return to God and take your place back. He hates you with a special hatred, and sooner or later, he will try to kill you. If God allows this to happen, you will be in his hell for eternity.

There are people who do not believe there is a hell. However, their unbelief does not make it any less real. If they are right and I live my life pure and holy, then when I die, I find out there is no hell, I have not lost anything. If I am right and they do not give themselves to the LORD, then they have an eternity to remember that someone loved them enough to tell them the truth yet they chose to go there. I don't even want to imagine what Satan has prepared for people like us. Hell was not created for humanity; it was prepared for Satan and his angels.

Every word of this book I have spoken in love for you. I understand your confusion. I understand the decision to give your life to the Lord is harder for you than someone who is straight. Yes, they have to change things in their lives, but you have to change everything in your life and yourself. I can tell you right now that you cannot do it. Only God can. You do not have to even try without him. Don't think you have to change first. You do not. You come just as you are; he will do the rest. He doesn't do it quickly, like yanking off a Band-Aid; he does it a little at a time. He promises he will not give you more than you can bear. He loves you more than you will ever know. It's not too late.

If you understand what I have written in this book, if you know in your heart it is for you, then please, give God a chance. He will fill you with joy, peace, and contentment. Let me help you take your rightful place on God's wall. Say this prayer, out loud, from your heart, and believe; it's that easy.

Prayer

Dear heavenly Father, thank you for not giving up on me. I believe that you are the God of all Gods and that you gave your Son, Jesus, on the cross for me. Jesus, I believe you are alive today and that going through you is the only way to heaven. I'm tired, Lord. Tired of living a lie. Tired of acting like I'm fulfilled and happy. I want to know what it is like to have peace, joy, and unconditional love.

Please, come into my heart; be my Lord and Savior. Wash my sins away, never to be remembered against me again. Fill me with your Holy Spirit and place me back on your wall. Thank you, Lord. In Jesus' name, I pray. Amen.

Congratulations! Find yourself a loving, spirit-filled church that teaches the Word of God. If you have a problem finding a church, watch TBN or Daystar, pray daily, and read your Bible, starting in Matthew. Get to know your Savior and Lord, Jesus Christ. There is one more thing I want you to remember: if you fail, do not give up. It does not mean you are lost; it simply means you have to go to the Lord and repent. He will forgive you if he knows you are truly sorry and that you do not want to repeat your failure. He loves you, and so do I.

I'll see you in heaven.

Praise God!

It's Only My Mercy

I have never questioned God's ability to recreate me into his likeness. Though I lived in sin many years and questioned God in other ways, I never doubted his love for me or his longing to have a relationship with me. Whether it was because of the miracles he had done in my life or the vision I had seen, I knew his love for me was real and inexhaustible.

I did not realize until years after I had been saved that I had a root of pride. Because of my godly heritage and my knowing of how much the LORD loved me, I had a false since of security. Part of me believed he would protect me, regardless of the depth of my sin. How arrogant and ignorant can a body be? I now realize he kept me through being shot twice, three tornadoes, and many other near death-encounters, not because I was somehow special, but because of his mercy. If it weren't for his mercy, I would be in hell today.

A few years ago, I was given a death sentence by my doctor. It was a diagnosis that has caused many people to take their own lives because of the fear it evokes. I left the doctor's office, stopped and told my aunt, stopped and told my mom, and then went home. I was not depressed, nor was I scared. I think I was numb, in shock.

The next morning, I got up, and as I started down the hallway to the living room, the words of my doctor rang in my ears, *You have stage four cancer of the intestines*. I remember feeling this horrible wave of fear start to grip me. It was a fear unlike any I have ever felt. I was totally consumed. Suddenly, I heard a familiar voice in my spirit say, "It's only my mercy." Before I reached the living room, the fear was gone and has never returned. Though I only felt that fear for a few seconds, I cannot imagine how anyone could stand it without Christ in their lives. It felt as if the fear alone could have killed me. Thank God I knew him and I knew his Word.

> For God hath not given us the spirit of fear; but of power, and of love, and of a sound mind.
>
> 2 Timothy 1:7

I ended up having to help others cope with the news. Instead of them giving me strength and words of comfort, I was giving it to them. God used me to show them how to walk through the valley of the shadow of death, how to be strong in the day of adversity, how to lean on and totally trust in him. God has taught me how to be dependent upon him. I have learned how to trust him for my every need. I have also realized how I can do nothing without him, including taking my next breath.

It has been almost five years since my diagnosis. I am no better, no worse; the LORD has sustained me. I believe this sickness will be used for his glory. I also believe in the healing power of Jesus Christ. I know he did not take the stripes on his back in vain. I believe it is for a higher purpose that shall be seen in his timing.

> But he was wounded for out transgressions, he was bruised for out iniquities the chastisement of our peace was upon him; and with his stripes we are healed.
>
> Isaiah 53:5

There are some who would believe that I am sick in my flesh because of my past sins.

> Be not deceived; God is not mocked: for whatsoever a man soweth, that shall he also reap. For he that soweth to his flesh shall of the flesh reap corruption (death):
>
> Galatians 6:7–8

It is impossible to threaten a Christian with death. If I leave my body, I will live eternally with my LORD in heaven. How is that a bad thing? How could that be repayment for my sins?

> ...but he that soweth to the Spirit shall of the Spirit reap life everlasting.

God allows us to suffer for different reasons.

1. *He allows suffering to produce fruit.*

My biggest regret, or fear, is not that I might die but that I would have to stand before my God without accomplishing my purpose and without bearing fruit. The thought of standing before him empty-handed after all he has done for me is unbearable. I cried out to him in my pain and discomfort and pleaded with him not to allow that to happen. It was only a few days later that he allowed me to start writing this book.

2. *He allows suffering for his glory.*

> 17-I shall not die, but live, and declare the works of the LORD.
> 18-The LORD hath chastened me sore: but he hath not given me over unto death.
>
> Psalm 118:17-18

> This sickness is not unto death, but for the glory of God, that the Son of God might be glorified (honored) thereby.
>
> John 11:4

The last verse is referring to Lazarus, who died and was raised from the dead for the glory of God. Jesus could have healed him before his death but did not. He waited in order to show the power of God.

3. *He allows suffering as a test of our faith.*

Will we grow angry with God? Will we stop believing his word? Will we question his love for us?

> Behold, I have refined thee, but not with silver; I have chosen thee in the furnace of affliction.
>
> Isaiah 49:10

> That the trial of your faith, being much more precious than of gold that perisheth, though it be tried by fire, might be found unto praise and honor and glory at the appearing of Jesus Christ.
>
> 1 Peter 1:7

4. *He allows suffering to teach us that we can do nothing without him.*

> My grace is sufficient for thee: for my strength is made perfect in weakness.
>
> 2 Corinthians 12:19

> For which cause we faint not; but though our outward man perish, yet the inward man is renewed day by day
>
> 2 Corinthians 4:16

5. *He allows suffering to prepare us to teach others.*

> Who comforteth us in all our tribulations, that we may be able to comfort them which are in any trouble, by the comfort wherewith we ourselves are comforted by God.
>
> 2 Corinthians 1:4

The LORD has taught me many things through my suffering. I'm sure he will teach me more. The biggest lesson I have learned is it's okay to be alone. There are times I am alone for a week or two at a time. Needless to say, my fear of being alone has been conquered. I now enjoy my time with him.

Although I look forward to the LORD healing me, I do so only to rid myself of the pain and discomfort. If I had a choice to go back five years ago and never have gotten sick or to keep all he has taught me and the relationship I have with him today, I would choose the pain, surgeries, discomfort, and solitude. Whether I am sick because of my sin or because the

LORD is teaching me to be more like him, it really doesn't matter anymore. I am now jealous of the thought of losing my time of isolation and dependency upon my LORD and Savior.

Isn't it ironic? It has taken severe mental, emotional, physical, and spiritual suffering to bring me to what was God's plan for me forty-eight years ago. I am now doing what he created me to do. I am his and his alone.

I am living the life of a nonsexual eunuch. I am more content, fulfilled, peaceful, and happier than I have ever been. I spend a lot of my time in study and prayer. I talk to the LORD daily. He knows I am here for him. Whether he needs an intercessor, a friend, a prayer warrior, or someone to share his heart with, he knows I am always available. He in return is always by my side. There are times I actually have to look to see whether he is standing next to me. His presence is that strong. I am having the best relationship I have ever had. I do not have to worry about infidelity, being lied to, stabbed in the back, or being rejected. I am unconditionally loved and never alone. I have found my soul mate, my greatest love, my best friend, and my reason for living. Everything I have ever wanted, I have found in him. After twenty years of rejection, fear, heartbreak, and shattered dreams, I now have all I was searching for.

The Bible says he will fulfill your hearts desires. He knows exactly what I want and what I need, because he is the one who created me and placed my desires within me. This means he will never disappoint or hurt me. He knows what I want before I even ask. He is my support, lover of my soul, and husband. He is my world.

A WORD TO THE SERVANTS OF GOD

If you are a minister or a Bible teacher, thank you for continuing to the end of this book. I know in reading it there have been several opportunities for you to become offended. There is, however, something I would like to speak to you, as a servant of the LORD.

If you have made it this far, it tells me you have a heart for the homosexual and for souls, in general. You also have a willingness to endure some hard criticism in order to understand how to reach them, arm yourself with the truth, and prepare to go to work with the appropriate tools, even though receiving them may have caused you some discomfort in being corrected so harshly. I hope you understand the urgency and spirit in which it was intended. Souls are my focus, not your feelings. I hope and pray you understand.

I want to tell you how much I love you and respect the work you do for Christ. There is not a man or woman who has preached the gospel who has not had to deny themselves and pay a price to carry the anointing of God.

For those who are still reading that are not called to some type of ministry, let me explain. Anytime someone is called to ministry, whether it is preaching, teaching, singing, writing, etc., they are added to the top of Satan's hit list. There is nothing he hates more than the word of God going forth. Why? Because Jesus is the word, and it is Jesus who has and will defeat him. Therefore, these people become the bull's-eye for his hatred.

You see them dressed nice, standing before the church, smiling, and looking like they have it all together. You don't understand the warfare they endure, the hours of study and prayer, and the many tears they have shed on their knees and on their face before God, crying out for the unsaved. They literally stand in the gap between God and Satan, pleading for your souls, warring off Satan's attacks, and receiving word, revelation, understanding, and wisdom for a hurting, dying world. Most of the time, they are not appreciated. More often than not, their names are not called out in prayer by others. Instead, they are talked about or forgotten until something happens and someone needs their prayers. Still, they are willing to pay the price in order to reach the lost for Christ.

So to all those who minister and teach God's word, I would like to take this opportunity to let you know how much I appreciate each and every one of you. Thank you for the sacrifice you have willingly become. It is people like you who have aided Christ in holding back the powers of Satan from destroying this world and all of humanity. I know you shall be richly rewarded.

So the question is, how do we successfully minister to the homosexual? Everyone knows you cannot harvest wheat with a cherry picker. You can't screw in a bolt with a hammer. You can't hammer in a nail with a socket wrench. In a sense, this is what has been happening. It has not happened, I pray, due to lack of compassion or mercy, but it is due to lack of understanding and knowledge on this subject. So let's go to our hardware provider, the Bible, and get some new tools to build a new sermon.

First, you must remember what I have told you. Though they were not actually born into homosexuality, they believe they were. This is what matters. It is all they have ever known; it's all they can remember. For this reason, there is something in them that blames God, since he is the one who created them. Whether this is true or not is not the question. It is how they feel. Therefore, it is where we have to start. Just as Moses was not born an Egyptian, it is all he knew; he couldn't remember life before. Did this make him Egyptian? No.

Second, all the people led out of Egypt were born slaves. They had a different mentality than Moses. Moses knew what it meant to be free. He knew what it was like to live in a type of the Promised Land. He lived as royalty in a place, if you will, that flowed with milk and honey, with every blessing he could think of. He knew and understood what he was trying to give to his people, how it would change their lives, and how much better they would feel, not just in their bodies, but in their minds. He understood the possibilities.

Not only had they lived their whole lives in Egypt, but Egypt was in them. Let's not forget that they, unlike today, did not have the power of the Holy Spirit living within them. Yes, they saw God do miraculous, wonderful things, but he was external, not internal. The difference between them and Moses was that Moses understood where he was taking them; yet, they couldn't comprehend it. All they knew was life in Egypt, life in bondage. Without the Holy Spirit, they didn't have the power to change.

Third, they couldn't understand how putting more rules and commands on them would make them free. They already lived with all the rules of the Egyptians. Now they were in the middle of nowhere, constantly being told what they could and could not do. They were told when to move, when to be still, what they could eat, how and when to worship, not to mention the Ten Commandments. To them, it felt as if they were still in bondage but under different taskmasters.

This is how the homosexual views Christianity. They feel as if they have to change their lives to live by a list of rules. They don't understand. They have to be taught, in depth, who the Holy Spirit is and what he does. Teach them that when he is present, it is his presence that makes you want to live clean, holy, and pure before God. They need to understand that when you are saved and filled with the Holy Spirit, there are no rules, only a way of life—a life of freedom, peace, and contentment. A life filled by the mercy and grace of God.

Finally, they have got to understand grace. There are people who have gone to church for years who still do not understand grace or mercy. They are still bound by legalism. They read the Bible, go to church, and try to do good, believing it will somehow get them to heaven. They do not understand that it is useless without a real relationship with the LORD.

Tell them who they are instead of who they are not. Help them to understand they are like the people led out of Egypt; they are a chosen people, created to be used of God. Let them know there are gifts and talents within them, placed there by God before they were born. Help them to understand how Satan changed their purpose into a lie, causing them to become the exact opposite of who God created them to be. Teach them how much God loves them. He loves them so much he created them different to be his and his alone. It's really very simple. Tell them the opposite of what they have heard: *the truth.*

I pray this book has been eye-opening without discouraging to you. It is not my intention to bring you down in the Spirit but to stir up the gifts that are in you with new understanding and excitement. It is my desire to open a new field with new tools to harvest a people who desperately need your love, compassion, and truth. Never underestimate the power of God to change and deliver these people into his likeness. They can add to your church when set free and filled with the Holy Spirit of the living God. Provide for them a place of belonging, a place of growth, and a place of healing. I have opened my heart to you to motivate you and allow you to see God is able to do the impossible, when given the chance. I am his proof that all sin can be defeated and all lives can be changed by the blood of Jesus.

May God bless and richly reward you.

Afterword

I have fought many battles, spent hours in prayer, suffered greatly in my body, and cried buckets of tears to receive the revelation of this book. I know as well as I know my name this is the word of God. I have paid the price. I have asked God to anoint it and use it for his glory. I don't want his glory. If there is one thing I do know, I know this is a word that Satan did not want released. He has tried several times to kill me. But I knew if it was of God, Satan would not prevail. Well, I'm still alive and praising God, though I need your prayers.

I have carried this book (this baby) in my spirit for twelve years. Like Elizabeth, this is an old pregnancy, only possible by the moving and workings of the Holy Spirit. As far as I know, it is the voice of one, crying in the wilderness. I do not believe the LORD could return without every field being appropriately and completely harvested. This field remains. With your help, it will soon be harvested with love and compassion.

I do not take lightly the responsibility I have been given in writing this book. Neither do I say it is the word of the LORD without fear and trembling. If I had refused to write it, the blood of the homosexual would be on my hands as I stand before God. Now I have done my part. I am passing it to you. My prayers are with you. May all you do, for the glory of God, be blessed. Let's fulfill the Great Commission given to us by our LORD and Savior, Jesus Christ.

ENDNOTES

1 James Strong, Strong's Exhaustive Concordance of the Bible (Nashville: Thomas Nelson Publishers, 1984), "Dictionary of The Hebrew Bible" pg. 106-eunuch.

2. James Strong, Strong's Exhaustive Concordance of the Bible (Nashville: Thomas Nelson Publishers, 1984), "Dictionary of The Hebrew Bible" pg. 47-knowledge.

3. Strong's Exhaustive Concordance, "Dictionary of The Hebrew Bible" pg. 52-law.

4. Strong's Exhaustive Concordance, "Dictionary of The Hebrew Bible" pg. 54-grievous.

5. Strong's Exhaustive Concordance, "Greek Dictionary of the New Testament", pg 77-grace.

6. Strong's Exhaustive Concordance, "Dictionary of The Hebrew Bible", pg 62-Midian.

7. Strong's Exhaustive Concordance, "Dictionary of The Hebrew Bible", pg 108-strife.

BIBLIOGRAPHY

Strong, James. The New Strong's Exhaustive Concordance of the Bible. Nashville: Thomas Nelson Publishers, 1984.

The Open Bible, Expanded Edition. King James Version. Riverside Book and Bible House. Iowa Falls: Thomas Nelson Publishers, 1985.